Augustus Hare

Sketches in Holland and Scandinavia

Augustus Hare

Sketches in Holland and Scandinavia

ISBN/EAN: 9783743321779

Manufactured in Europe, USA, Canada, Australia, Japa

Cover: Foto ©ninafisch / pixelio.de

Manufactured and distributed by brebook publishing software (www.brebook.com)

Augustus Hare

Sketches in Holland and Scandinavia

SKETCHES

IN

HOLLAND AND SCANDINAVIA

BY

AUGUSTUS J. C. HARE

AUTHOR OF "CITIES OF ITALY," "WANDERINGS IN SPAIN," ETC.

LONDON
GEORGE ALLEN, 156, CHARING CROSS ROAD
[*All rights reserved*]

PREFACE.

THE slight sketches in this volume are only the result of ordinary tours in the countries they attempt to describe. Yet the days they recall were so delightful, and their memory—especially of the tour in Norway—is so indescribably sunny, that I cannot help hoping their publication may lead others to enjoy what is at once so pleasant and so easy of attainment.

AUGUSTUS J. C. HARE.

HOLMHURST : *November* 1884.

CONTENTS.

IN HOLLAND.

IN DENMARK.

IN SWEDEN.

IN NORWAY.

IN HOLLAND

B

IN HOLLAND.

AT Roosendal, about an hour's railway journey from Antwerp, the boundary between Belgium and Holland is crossed, and a branch line diverges to Breda.

Somehow, like most travellers, we could not help expecting to see some marked change on reaching a new country, and in Holland one could not repress the expectation of beginning at once to see the pictures of Teniers and Gerard Dou in real life. We were certainly disappointed at first. Open heaths were succeeded by woods of stunted firs, and then by fields with thick hedges of beech or alder, till the towers of Breda came in sight. Here a commonplace omnibus took us to the comfortable inn of Zum Kroon, and we were shown into bedrooms reached by an open wooden staircase from the courtyard, and quickly joined the table d'hôte, at which the magnates of the town were seated with napkins well tucked up under their chins, talking, with full mouths, in Dutch, of which to our unaccustomed ears the words seemed all in one string. Most excellent was the dinner—roast meat and pears, quantities of delicious vegetables cooked in different ways, piles of ripe mulberries and cake, and across the little garden, with its statues and bright flower-beds, we could see the red sails of the barges going up and down the canals.

As soon as dinner was over, we sallied forth to see the town, which impressed us more than any Dutch city did afterwards, perhaps because it was the first we saw. The winding streets—one of them ending in a high windmill—are lined with houses wonderfully varied in outline, and of every shade of delicate colour, yellow, grey, or brown, though the windows always have white frames and bars. Passing through a low archway under one of the houses, we found ourselves, when we least expected it, in the public garden, a kind of wood where the trees have killed all the grass, surrounded by canals, beyond one of which is a great square château built by William III. of England, encircled by the Merk, and enclosing an arcaded court. There was an older château of 1350 at Breda, but we failed to find it.

In stately splendour, from the old houses of the market-place, rises the noble Hervormde Kerk (Protestant Church), with a lofty octagon tower, and a most characteristic bulbous Dutch spire. Here, as we wanted to see the interior, we first were puzzled by our ignorance of Dutch, finding, as everywhere in the smaller towns, that the natives knew no language but their own. But two old women in high caps and gold earrings observed our puzzledom from a window

THE MARKET-PLACE AT BREDA.

and pointed to a man and a key—we nodded; the man pointed to himself, a door, and a key—we nodded; and we were soon inside the building. It was our first introduction to Dutch Calvinism and iconoclasm, and piteous indeed was it to see so magnificent a church thickly covered with whitewash, and the quantity of statues which it contains of deceased Dukes and Duchesses of Nassau bereft of their legs and petticoats. Only, in a grand side chapel on the left of the choir, the noble tomb of Engelbrecht II. of Nassau, general under the Emperor Maximilian (1505), remains intact. The guide lights matches to shine through the transparent alabaster of the figures; that of the Duke represents Death, that of the Duchess Sleep, as they lie beneath a stone slab which bears the armour of Engelbrecht, and is supported by figures of Cæsar, Hannibal, Regulus, and Philip of Macedon; that of Cæsar is sublime. The tomb of Sir Francis Vere in Westminster Abbey is of the same design, and is supposed to be copied from this famous monument. Outside the chapel is the tomb of Engelbrecht V. of Nassau, with all his family kneeling, in quaint headdresses. The other sights of the church are the brass font in the Baptistery, and a noble brass in the choir of William de Gaellen, Dean of the Chapter, 1539. It will be observed that here, and almost everywhere else in Holland, the names of saints which used to be attached to the churches have disappeared; the buildings are generally known as the old church, or new church, or great church.

After a delicious breakfast of coffee and thick

cream, with rusks, scones, and different kinds of cheese, always an indispensable in Dutch breakfasts, we took to the railway again and crossed Zealand, which chiefly consists of four islands, Noordt Beveland, Zuid Beveland, Schouwen, and Walcheren, and is less visited by the rest of the Netherlanders than any other part of the country. The land is all cut up into vast polders, as the huge meadows are called, which are recovered from the sea and protected by embankments. Here, if human care was withdrawn for six months, the whole country would be under the sea again. A corps of engineers called 'waterstaat' are continually employed to watch the waters, and to keep in constant repair the dykes, which are formed of clay at the bottom, as that is more waterproof than anything else, and thatched with willows, which are here grown extensively for the purpose. If the sea passes a dyke, ruin is imminent, an alarm bell rings, and the whole population rush to the rescue. The moment one dyke is even menaced, the people begin to build another inside it, and then rely upon the double defence, whilst they fortify the old one. But all their care has not preserved the islands of Zealand. Three centuries ago, Schouwen was entirely submerged, and every living creature was drowned. Soon after, Noordt Beveland was submerged, and remained for several years entirely under water, only the points of the church spires being visible. Zuid Beveland had been submerged in the fourteenth century. Walcheren was submerged as late as 1808, and Tholen even in 1825. It has been aptly asserted that the sea to the inhabitants of

BERGEN-OP-ZOOM.

Holland is what Vesuvius is to Torre del Greco. How well its French name of Pays-Bas suits the country! De Amicis says that the Dutch have three enemies— the sea, the lakes, and the rivers; they repel the sea, they dry the lakes, and they imprison the rivers; but with the sea it is a combat which never ceases.

The story of the famous siege of 1749 made us linger at Bergen-op-Zoom, a clean, dull little town with bright white houses surrounding an irregular market-place, and surmounted by the heavy tower of the Church of S. Gertrude. In the Stadhuis is a fine carved stone chimney-piece; but there is little worth seeing, and we were soon speeding across the rich pastures of Zuid Beveland, and passing its capital of Goes, prettily situated amongst cherry orchards, the beautiful cruciform church with a low central spire rising above the trees on its ramparts. Every now and then the train seems scarcely out of the water, which covers a vast surface of the pink-green flats, and recalls the description in Hudibras of—

> A country that draws fifty feet of water,
> In which men live as in the hold of nature,
> And when the sea does in upon them break,
> And drown a province, does but spring a leak.

The peasant women at the stations are a perpetual amusement, for there is far more costume here than in most parts of Holland, and peculiar square handsome gold ornaments, something like closed golden books, are universally worn on each side of the face.

So, crossing a broad salt canal into the island of Walcheren, we reached Middleburg, a handsome town which was covered with water to the house tops when the island was submerged. It was the birthplace of Zach Janssen and Hans Lipperhey, the inventors of the telescope, *c.* 1610. In the market-place is a most beautiful Gothic townhall, built by the architect Keldermans, early in the sixteenth century. We asked a well dressed boy how we could get into it, and he, without further troubling himself, pointed the way with his finger. The building contains a quaint old hall called the Vierschaar, and a so-called museum, but there is little enough to see. As we came out the boy met us. 'You must give me something: I pointed out the entrance of the Stadhuis to you.' In Holland we have always found that no one, rich or poor, does a kindness or even a civility for nothing!

The crowd in the market-place was so great that it was impossible to sketch the Stadhuis as we should have wished, but the people themselves were delightfully picturesque. The women entirely conceal their hair under their white caps, but have golden corkscrews sticking out on either side the face, like weapons of defence, from which the golden slabs we have observed before were pendant. The Nieuwe Kerk is of little interest, though it contains the tomb of William of Holland, who was elected Emperor of Germany in 1250, and we wandered on through the quiet streets,

DORTRECHT.

till a Gothic arch in an ancient wall looked tempting. Passing through it we found ourselves in the enclosure of the old abbey, shaded by a grove of trees, and surrounded by ancient buildings, part of which are appropriated as the Hotel Abdij, where we arrived utterly famished, and found a table d'hôte at 2.30 P.M. unspeakably reviving.

Any one who sees Holland thoroughly ought also to visit Zieriksee, the capital of the island of Schouwen; but the water locomotion thither is so difficult and tedious that we preferred keeping to the railways, which took us back in the dark over the country we had already traversed, and a little more, to Dortrecht, where there is a convenient tramway to take travellers from the station into the town. Here, at the Hôtel de Fries, we found comfortable bedrooms, with boarded floors and box-beds like those in Northumbrian cottages, and we had supper in the public room, separated into two parts by a daïs for strangers, whence we looked down into the humbler division, which recalled many homely scenes of Ostade and Teniers in its painted wooden ceiling, its bright, polished furniture, its cat and dog and quantity of birds and flowers, its groups of boors at round tables drinking out of tankards, and the landlady and her daughter in their gleaming gold ornaments, sitting knitting, with the waiter standing behind them amusing himself by the general conversation.

Our morning at Dortrecht was very delightful, and it is a thoroughly charming place. Passing under a dark archway in a picturesque building of Charles V. opposite the hotel, we found ourselves at once on the edge of an immense expanse of shimmering river, with long rich polders beyond, between which the wide flood breaks into three different branches. Red and white sails flit down them. Here and there rise a line of pollard willows or clipped elms, and now and then a church spire. On the nearest shore an ancient windmill, coloured in delicate tints of grey and yellow, surmounts a group of white buildings. On the left is a broad esplanade of brick, lined with ancient houses, and a canal with a bridge, the long arms of which are ready to open at a touch and give a passage to the great yellow-masted barges, which are already half intercepting the bright red house-fronts ornamented with stone, which belong to some public buildings facing the end of the canal. With what a confusion of merchandise are the boats laden, and how gay is the colouring, between the old weedy posts to which they are moored!

It was from hence that Isabella of France, with Sir John de Hainault and many other faithful knights, set out on their expedition against Edward II. and the government of the Spencers.

From the busy port, where nevertheless they are dredging, we cross another bridge and find ourselves in a quietude like that of a cathedral close in England. On one side is a wide pool half covered with floating timber, and, in the other half, reflecting like a mirror the houses on the opposite shore, with their bright gardens of lilies and hollyhocks, and trees of mountain ash, which bend their masses of scarlet berries to the still water. Between the houses are glints of blue river and of inevitable windmills on the opposite shore. And all this we observe standing in the shadow of a huge church, the Groote Kerk, with a nave of the fourteenth century, and a choir of the fifteenth, and a gigantic brick tower, in which three long Gothic arches, between octagonal tourelles, enclose several tiers of windows. At the top is a great clock, and below the church a grove of elms, through which fitful sunlight falls on the grass and the dead red of the brick pavement (so grateful to feet sore with the sharp stones of other Dutch cities), where groups of fishermen are collecting in their blue shirts and white trousers.

There is little to see inside this or any other church in Holland; travellers will rather seek for the memorials, at the Kloveniers Doelen, of the famous Synod of Dort, which was held 1618-19, in the hope of effecting a compromise between the Gomarists, or disciples of Calvin, and the Arminians who followed Zwingli, and who had recently obtained the name of

GROOTE KERK, DORTRECHT.

Remonstrants from the 'remonstrance' which they had addressed eight years before in defence of their doctrines. The Calvinists held that the greater part of mankind was excluded from grace, which the

Arminians denied; but at the Synod of Dort the Calvinists proclaimed themselves as infallible as the Pope, and their resolutions became the law of the Dutch reformed Church. The Arminians were forthwith outlawed; a hundred ministers who refused to subscribe to the dictates of the Synod were banished;

CANAL AT DORTRECHT.

Hugo Grotius and Rombout Hoogerbeets were imprisoned for life at Loevestein; the body of the secretary Ledenberg, who committed suicide in prison, was hung; and Van Olden Barneveldt, the friend of William the Silent, was beheaded in his seventy-second year.

There is nothing in the quiet streets of Dortrecht to remind one that it was once one of the most important commercial cities of Holland, taking precedence even of Rotterdam, Delft, Leyden, and Amsterdam. It also possessed a privilege called the Staple of Dort, by which all the carriers on the Maas and Rhine were forced to unload their merchandise here, and pay all duties imposed, only using the boats or porters of the place in their work, and so bringing a great revenue to the town.

More than those in any of the other towns of Holland do the little water streets of Dortrecht recall Venice, the houses rising abruptly from the canals; only the luminous atmosphere and the shimmering water changing colour like a chameleon, are wanting.

Through the street of wine—Wijnstraat—built over storehouses used for the staple, we went to the Museum to see the pictures. There were two schools of Dortrecht. Jacob Geritse Cuyp (1575), Albert Cuyp (1605), Ferdinand Bol (1611), Nicolas Maas (1632), and Schalken (1643) belonged to the former; Arend de Gelder, Arnold Houbraken, Dirk Stoop, and Ary Scheffer are of the latter. Sunshine and glow were the characteristics of the first school, greyness and sobriety of the second. But there are few good pictures at Dort now, and some of the best

works of Cuyp are to be found in our National
Gallery, executed at his native place and portraying
the great brick tower of the church in the golden
haze of evening, seen across rich pastures, where the
cows are lying deep in the meadow grass. The works
of Ary Scheffer are now the most interesting pictures
in the Dortrecht Gallery. Of the subject 'Christus
Consolator' there are two representations. In the
more striking of these the pale Christ is seated
amongst the sick, sorrowful, blind, maimed, and en-
slaved, who are all stretching out their hands to Him.
Beneath is the tomb which the artist executed for his
mother, Cornelia Scheffer, whose touching figure is
represented lying with outstretched hands, in the
utmost abandonment of repose.

An excursion should be made from Dortrecht to
the castle of Loevestein on the Rhine, where Grotius,
imprisoned in 1619, was concealed by his wife in the
chest which brought in his books and linen. It was
conveyed safely out of the castle by her courageous
maid Elsje van Houwening, and was taken at first to
the house of Jacob Daatselaer, a supposed friend of
Grotius, who refused to render any assistance. But
his wife consented to open the chest, and the philosopher, disguised as a mason, escaped to Brabant.

It is much best to visit Rotterdam as an excursion

from Dortrecht. We thought it the most odious place we ever were in—immense, filthy, and not very picturesque. Its handsomest feature is the vast quay called the Boompjes, on the Maas. Here and there a great windmill reminds you unmistakably of where you are, and the land streets are intersected everywhere by water streets, the carriages being constantly stopped to let ships pass through the bridges. In the Groote Markt stands a bronze statue of Desiderius Erasmus—'Vir saeculi sui primarius, et civis omnium praestantissimus,' which is the work of Hendrik de Keyser (1662), and in the Wijde Kerkstraat is the house where he was born, inscribed 'Haec est parva domus, magnus qua natus Erasmus, 1467,' but it is now a tavern. The great church of S. Lawrence— Groote Kerk—built in 1477–87, contains the tombs of a number of Dutch admirals, and has a grand pavement of monumental slabs, but is otherwise frightful. The portion used for service is said to be 'so conveniently constructed that the zealous Christians of Rotterdam prefer sleeping through a sermon there, to any other church in the city.' Part of the rest is used as a cart-house, the largest chapel is a commodious carpenter's shop, and the aisles round the part which is still a church, where there has been an attempt at restoration in painting the roof yellow and putting up some hideous yellow seats, are a playground for the children of the town, who are freely admitted in their perambulators, though for strangers there is a separate fee for each part of the edifice they enter.

We went to see the pictures in the Museum bequeathed to the town by Jacob Otto Boyman, but did not admire them much. It takes time to accustom one's mind to Dutch art, and the endless representations of family life, with domestic furniture, pots and pans, &c., or of the simple local landscapes—clipped avenues, sandy roads, dykes, and cottages, or even of the cows, and pigs, and poultry, which seem wonderfully executed, but, where one has too much of the originals, scarcely worth the immense amount of time and labour bestowed upon them. The calm seas of Van de Welde and Van der Capelle only afford a certain amount of relief. The scenes of village life are seldom pleasing, often coarse, and never have anything elevating to offer or ennobling to recall. We thought that the real charm of the Dutch school to outsiders consists in the immense power and variety of its portraits.

Hating Rotterdam, we thankfully felt ourselves speeding over the flat, rich lands to Gouda, where we found an agricultural fête going on, banners half way down the houses, and a triumphal arch as the entrance to the square, formed of spades, rakes, and forks, with a plough at the top, and decorated with corn, potatoes, turnips, and carrots, and cornucopias pouring out flowers at the sides. In the square—a great cheese market, for the Gouda cheese is esteemed the best in Holland—is a Gothic Stadhuis, and beyond it, the Groote Kerk of 1552, of which the bare interior is enlivened by the stained windows executed by Wonter and Dirk Crabeth in 1555-57. We were the better able to understand the design of these noble windows because the cartoon for each was spread upon the pavement in front of it; but one could not help one's attention being unpleasantly distracted by the number of men of the burgher class, smoking and with their hats on, who were allowed to use the church as a promenade. Gouda also made an unpleasant impression upon us, because, expensive as we found every hotel in Holland, we were nowhere so outrageously cheated as here.

It is a brief journey to the Hague—La Haye, Gravenhage—most delightful of little capitals, with its comfortable hotels and pleasant surroundings. The town is still so small that it seems to merit the name of 'the largest village in Europe,' which was given to it because the jealousy of other towns prevented its having any vote in the States General till the time of

Louis Bonaparte, who gave it the privileges of a city. It is said that the Hague, more than any other place, may recall what Versailles was just before the great revolution. It has thoroughly the aspect of a little royal city. Without any of the crowd and bustle of Amsterdam and Rotterdam, it is not dead like the

THE VIJVER.

smaller towns of Holland; indeed, it even seems to have a quiet gaiety, without dissipation, of its own. All around are parks and gardens, whence wide streets lead speedily through the new town of the rich bourgeoisie to the old central town of stadholders, where a beautiful lake, the Vijver, or fish-pond, comes as a surprise, with the eccentric old palace of the Binnenhof rising straight out of its waters. We had been told it was picturesque, but were prepared for nothing so charming as the variety of steep roofs and towers, the clear reflections, the tufted islet, and the beautiful colouring of the whole scene of the Vijver. Skirting the lake, we entered the precincts of the palace through the picturesque Gudevangen Poort, where Cornelius de Witte, Burgomaster of Dort, was imprisoned in 1672, on a false accusation of having suborned the surgeon William Tichelaur to murder the Prince of Orange. He was dragged out hence and torn to pieces by the people, together with his brother Jean de Witte, Grand Pensioner, whose house remains hard by in the Kneuterdijk.

The court of the Binnenhof is exceedingly handsome, and contains the ancient Gothic Hall of the Knights, where Johann van Olden Barneveld, Grand Pensioner, or Prime Minister, was condemned to death ' for having conspired to dismember the States of the Netherlands, and greatly troubled God's Church,' and in the front of which (May 24, 1619) he was beheaded.

Close to the north-east gate of the Binnenhof is the handsome house called Mauritshuis, containing the inestimable Picture Gallery of the Hague, which will bear many visits, and has the great charm of not being huge beyond the powers of endurance. On the ground floor are chiefly portraits, amongst which a simple dignified priest by Philippe de Champaigne, with a far-away expression, will certainly arrest attention. Deeply interesting is the portrait by Ravesteyn of William the Silent, in his ruff and steel armour

HALL OF THE KNIGHTS, THE HAGUE.

embossed with gold—a deeply lined face, with a slight peaked beard. His widow, Louise de Coligny, is also represented. There is a fine portrait by Schalcken of our William the Third. Noble likenesses of Sir George Sheffield and his wife Anna Wake, by Vandyke, are a pleasing contrast to the many works of

Rubens. There are deeply interesting portraits by Albert Dürer and Holbein.

On the first floor we must sit down before the great picture which Rembrandt painted in his twenty-sixth year (1632) of the School of Anatomy. Here the shrewd professor, Nicholaus Tulp, with a face brimming with knowledge and intelligence, is expounding the anatomy of a corpse to a number of members of the guild of surgeons, some of whom are full of eager interest and inquiry, whilst others are inattentive: the dead figure is greatly foreshortened and not repulsive. In another room, a fine work of Thomas de Keyser represents the Four Burgomasters of Amsterdam hearing of the arrival of Marie de Medicis. A beautiful work of Adrian van Ostade is full of light and character—but only represents a stolid boor drinking to the health of a fiddler, while a child plays with a dog in the background.

A group of admirers will always be found round 'the Immortal Bull' of Paul Potter, which was considered the fourth picture in importance in the Louvre, when the spoils of Europe were collected at Paris. De Amicis says, 'It lives, it breathes; with his bull Paul Potter has written the true Idyl of Holland.' It is, however—being really a group of cattle—not a pleasing, though a life-like picture. Much more attractive is the exquisite 'Presentation' of Rembrandt (1631), in which Joseph and Mary, simple peasants, present the Holy Child to Simeon, a glorious old man in a jewelled robe, who invokes a blessing upon the infant, while other priests look on with interest. A wonderful ray of light, falling upon the principal group, illuminates the whole temple. Perhaps the most beautiful work in the whole gallery is the Young Housekeeper of Gerard Dou. A lovely young woman sits at work by an open window looking into a street. By her side is the baby asleep in its cradle, over which the maid is leaning. The light falls on the chandelier and all the household belongings of a well-to-do citizen: in all there is the same marvellous finish; it is said that the handle of the broom took three days to paint.

There is not much to discover in the streets of the Hague. In the great square called the Plein is the statue of William the Silent, with his finger raised, erected in 1848 'by the grateful people to the father of their fatherland.' In the fish-market, tame storks are kept, for the same reason that bears are kept at Berne, because storks are the arms of the town. But the chief attraction of the place lies in its lovely walks amid the noble beeches and oaks of the Bosch, beyond which on the left is Huis ten Bosch, the Petit Trianon of the Hague, the favourite palace of Queen

Sophie, who held her literary court and died there. It is a quiet country house, looking out upon flats, with dykes and a windmill. All travellers seem to visit it, —which must be a ceaseless surprise to the extortionate custode to whom they have to pay a gulden a head, and who will hurry them rapidly through some commonplace rooms in which there is nothing really worth seeing. One room is covered with paintings of the

SCHEVENINGEN.

Rubens school, amid which, high in the dome, is a portrait of the Princess Amalia of Solms, who built the house in 1647.

A tram takes people for twopence halfpenny to Scheveningen through the park, a thick wood with charming forest scenery. As the trees become more scattered, the roar of the North Sea is heard upon the shore. Above the sands, on the dunes or sand-hills, which extend from the Helder to Dunkirk, is a broad terrace, lined on one side by a row of wooden pavilions with flags and porticoes, and below it are long lines of tents, necessary in the intense glare, while, nearer the waves, are thousands of beehive-like refuges, with a single figure seated in each. The flat monotonous shore would soon pall upon one, yet through the whole summer it is an extraordinary lively scene. The placid happiness of Dutch family life has here taken possession. On Sunday afternoons, especially, the sands seem as crowded with human existence as they are represented in the picture of Lingelbach, which we have seen in the Mauritshuis, portraying the vast multitude assembled here to witness the embarkation of Charles II. for England.

An excursion must be made to Delft, only twenty minutes distant from the Hague by rail. Pepys calls it 'a most sweet town, with bridges and a river in every street,' and that is a tolerably accurate description. It seems thinly inhabited, and the Dutch themselves look upon it as a place where one will die of *ennui*. It has scarcely changed with two hundred years. The view of Delft by Van der Meer in the Museum at the Hague might have been painted yesterday. All the trees are clipped, for in artificial Holland every work of Nature is artificialised. At certain seasons, numbers of storks may be seen upon the chimney-tops, for Delft is supposed to be the stork town *par excellence*. Near the shady canal Oude Delft is a low building, once the Convent of S. Agata, with an ornamented door surmounted by a relief, leading

ENTRANCE TO S. AGATA, DELFT.

into a courtyard. It is a common barrack now, for Holland, which has no local histories, has no regard whatever for its historic associations or monuments. Yet this is the greatest shrine of Dutch history, for it is here that William the Silent died.

Philip II. had promised 25,000 crowns of gold to any one who would murder the Prince of Orange. An attempt had already been made, but had failed, and William refused to take any measures for self-protection, saying, 'It is useless: my years are in the hands of God: if there is a wretch who has no fear of death, my life is in his hand, however I may guard it.' At length, a young man of seven-and-twenty appeared at Delft, who gave himself out to be one Guyon, a Protestant, son of Pierre Guyon, executed at Besançon for having embraced Calvinism, and declared that he was exiled for his religion. Really he was Balthazar Gerard, a bigoted Catholic, but his conduct in Holland soon procured him the reputation of an evangelical saint. The Prince took him into his service and sent him to accompany a mission from the States of Holland to the Court of France, whence he returned to bring the news of the death of the Duke of Anjou to William. At that time the Prince was living with his court in the convent of S. Agata, where he received Balthazar alone in his chamber. The moment was opportune, but the would-be assassin had no arms ready. William gave him a small sum of money and bade him hold himself in readiness to be sent back to France. With the money Balthazar bought two pistols from a soldier (who afterwards killed himself when he heard the use which was made of the purchase). On the next day, June 10, 1584, Balthazar returned to the convent as William was descending the staircase to dinner, with his fourth wife, Louise de Coligny (daughter of the Admiral who fell in the massacre of S. Bartholomew), on his arm. He presented his passport and begged the Prince to sign it, but was told to return later. At dinner the Princess asked William who was the young man who had spoken to him, for his expression was the most terrible she had ever seen. The Prince laughed, said it was Guyon, and was as gay as usual. Dinner being over, the family party were about to remount the staircase. The assassin was waiting in a dark corner at the foot of the stairs, and as William passed he discharged a pistol with three balls and fled. The Prince staggered, saying, 'I am wounded; God have mercy upon me and my poor people.' His sister Catherine van Schwartzbourg asked, 'Do you trust in Jesus Christ?' He said, 'Yes,' with a feeble voice, sat down upon the stairs, and died.

Balthazar reached the rampart of the town in safety, hoping to swim to the other side of the moat, where a horse awaited him. But he had dropped his hat and his second pistol in his flight, and so he was traced and seized before he could leap from the wall.

Amid horrible tortures, he not only confessed, but continued to triumph in his crime. His judges believed him to be possessed of the devil. The next day he was executed. His right hand was burnt off in a tube of red-hot iron: the flesh of his arms and legs was torn off with red-hot pincers; but he never made a cry. It was not till his breast was cut open, and his heart torn out and flung in his face, that he expired. His head was then fixed on a pike, and his body cut into four quarters, exposed on the four gates of the town.

Close to the Prinsenhof is the Oude Kerk with a leaning tower. It is arranged like a very ugly theatre inside, but contains, with other tombs of celebrities, the monument of Admiral van Tromp, 1650—'Martinus Harberti Trompius'—whose effigy lies upon his back, with swollen feet. It was this Van Tromp who defeated the English fleet under Blake, and perished, as represented on the monument, in an engagement off Scheveningen. It was he who, after his victory over the English, caused a broom to be hoisted at his mast-head to typify that he had swept the Channel clear of his enemies.

The Nieuwe Kerk in the Groote Markt (1412-76) contains the magnificent monument of William the Silent by Hendrik de Keyser and A. Quellin (1621).

Black marble columns support a white canopy over the white sleeping figure of the Prince, who is represented in his little black silk cap, as he is familiar to us in his pictures. In the recesses of the tomb— —'*somptueux et tourmenté*,' as Montégut calls it—are statues of Liberty, Justice, Prudence, and Religion. At the feet of William lies his favourite dog, which saved his life from midnight assassins at Malines, by awakening him. At the head of the tomb is another figure of William, of bronze, seated. In the same church is a monument to Hugo Grotius —' prodigium Europae '—the greatest lawyer of the seventeenth century, presented to Henri IV. by Barneveld as ' La merveille de la Hollande.'

On leaving the Hague a few hours should be given to the dull university town of Leyden, unless it has been seen as an afternoon excursion from the capital. This melancholy and mildewed little town, mouldering from a century of stagnation, the birthplace of Rembrandt, surrounds the central tower of its Burg—standing in the grounds of an inn, which exacts payment from those who visit it. Close by is the huge church of S. Pancras—Houglansche Kerk — of the fifteenth century, containing the tomb of Van der Werff, burgomaster during the famous siege, who answered the starving people, when they came demanding bread or surrender, that he had 'sworn to defend the city, and, with God's help, he meant to keep his oath, but that if his body would help them to prolong the defence, they might take it and share it amongst those who were most hungry.' A covered bridge over a canal leads to the Bredenstrasse, where there is a picturesque grey stone Stadhuis of the sixteenth century. It contains the principal work of Cornelius Engelbrechtsen of Leyden (1468-1533), one of the earliest of Dutch painters—an altarpiece representing the Crucifixion, with the Sacrifice of Abraham and Worship of the Brazen Serpent in the side panels, as symbols of the Atonement: on the pedestal is a naked body, out of which springs a tree—the tree of life—and beside it kneel the donors. The neighbouring church of S. Peter (1315) contains the tomb of Boerhaave, the physician, whose lectures in the University were attended by Peter the Great, and for whom a Chinese mandarin found 'à l'illustre M. Boerhaave, médecin, en Europe,' quite sufficient direction. Boerhaave was the doctor who said that the poor were his best patients, for God paid for them.

The streets are grass-grown, the houses damp, the canals green with weed. The University has fallen into decadence since others were established at

Utrecht, Groningen, and Amsterdam; but Leyden is still the most flourishing of the four. When William of Orange offered the citizens freedom from taxes, as a reward for their endurance of the famous siege, they thanked him, but said they would rather have a university. Grotius and Cartesius (Descartes), Arminius and Gomar, were amongst its professors, and the University possesses an admirable botanical museum and a famous collection of Japanese curiosities.

The Rhine cuts up the town of Leyden into endless islands, connected by a hundred and fifty bridges. On a quiet canal near the Beesten Markt is the Museum, which contains the 'Last Judgment' of Lucas van Leyden (1494-1533), a scholar of Engelbrechtsen, and one of the patriarchs of Dutch painting.

A few minutes bring us from Leyden to Haarlem by the railway. It crosses an isthmus between the sea and a lake which covered the whole country between Leyden, Haarlem, and Amsterdam till 1839, when it became troublesome, and the States-General forthwith, after the fashion of Holland, voted its destruction. Enormous engines were at once employed to drain it by pumping the water into canals, which carried it to the sea, and the country was the richer by a new province.

Haarlem, on the river Spaarne, stands out distinct in recollection from all other Dutch towns, for it has the most picturesque market-place in Holland—the Groote Markt—surrounded by quaint houses of varied outline, amidst which rises the Groote Kerk

MARKET-PLACE, HAARLEM.

of S. Bavo, a noble cruciform fifteenth-century building. The interior, however, is as bare and hideous as all other Dutch churches. It contains a monument to the architect Conrad, designer of the famous locks of Katwijk, 'the defender of Holland against the fury of the sea and the power of tempests.' Behind the choir is the tomb of the poet Bilderdijk, who only died in 1831, and near this the grave of Laurenz Janzoom—the Coster or Sacristan —who is asserted in his native town, but never believed outside it, to have been the real inventor of printing, as he is said to have cut out letters in wood, and taken impressions from them in ink, as early as 1423. His partisans also maintain that whilst he was attending a midnight mass, praying for patience to endure the ill-treatment of his enemies, all his implements were stolen, and that when he found this out on his return he died of grief. It is further declared that the robber was Faust of Mayence, the brother of Gutenberg, and that it was thus that the honour of the invention passed from Holland to Germany, where Gutenberg produced his invention of movable type twelve years later. There is a statue of the Coster in front of the church, and, on its north side, his house is preserved and adorned with his bust.

Amongst a crowd of natives with their hats on, talking in church as in the market-place, we waited to hear the famous organ of Christian Muller (1735-38), and grievously were we disappointed with its discordant noises. All the men smoked in church, and this we saw repeatedly; but it would be difficult to say where we ever saw a Dutchman with a pipe out of his mouth. Every man seemed to be systematically smoking away the few wits he possessed.

Opposite the Groote Kerk is the Stadhuis, an old palace of the Counts of Holland remodelled. It contains a delightful little gallery of the works of Franz Hals, which at once transports the spectator into the Holland of two hundred years ago— such is the marvellous variety of life and vigour impressed into its endless figures of stalwart officers and handsome young archers pledging each other at banquet tables and seeming to welcome the visitor with jovial smiles as he enters the chamber, or of serene old ladies, 'regents' of hospitals, seated at their council boards. The immense power of the artist is shown in nothing so much as in the hands, often gloved, dashed in with instantaneous power, yet always having the effect of the most consummate finish at a distance. Behind one of the pictures is the entrance to the famous 'secret-room of Haarlem,' seldom seen, but containing an inestimable collection of historic relics of the time of the famous siege of Leyden.

April and May are the best months for visiting Haarlem, which is the bulb nursery garden of the world. 'Oignons à fleurs' are advertised for sale everywhere. Tulips are more cultivated than any other flowers, as ministering most to the national craving for colour; but times are changed since a single bulb of the tulip 'L'Amiral Liefkenshoch' sold for 4,500 florins, one of 'Viceroy' for 4,200, and one of 'Semper Augustus' for 13,000.

Now we entered Amsterdam, to which we had looked forward as the climax of our tour, having read of it and pondered upon it as 'the Venice of the north;' but our expectations were raised much too high. Anything more unlike Venice it would be difficult to imagine: and there is a terrible want of variety and colour; many of the smaller towns of Holland are far more interesting and infinitely more picturesque.

A castle was built at Amsterdam in 1204, but the town only became important in the sixteenth century, since which it has been the most commercial of ancient European cities. It is situated upon the influx of the Amstel to the Y, as the arm of the Zuider Zee which forms the harbour is called, and it occupies a huge semicircle, its walls being enclosed by the broad moat, six and a half miles long, which is known as Buitensingel. The greater part of the houses are built on piles, causing Erasmus to say that the inhabitants lived on trees like rooks. In the centre of the town is the great square called Dam, one side of which is occupied by the handsome Royal Palace—Het Palais—built by J. van Kampen in 1648. The Nieuwe Kerk (1408–1470) contains a number of monuments to admirals, including those of Van Ruiter—'immensi tremor oceani'—who com-

MILL NEAR AMSTERDAM.

manded at the battle of Solbay, and Van Speyk, who blew himself up with his ship in 1831, rather than yield to the Belgians. In the Oude Kerk of 1300 there are more tombs of admirals. Hard by, in the Nieuwe Markt, is the picturesque cluster of fifteenth-century towers called S. Anthonieswaag, once a city gate and now a weighing-house.

But the great attraction of Amsterdam is the Picture Gallery of the Trippenhuis, called the Rijks Museum, and it deserves many visits. Amongst the portraits in the first room we were especially attracted by that of William the Silent in his skull-cap, by Miereveld, but all the House of Orange are represented here from the first to the last We also see all the worthies of the nation—Ruyter, Van Tromp and his wife, Grotius and his wife, Johann and Cornelis de Witt, Johann van Oldenharneveldt, and his wife Maria of Utrecht, a peaceful old lady in a ruff and brown dress edged with fur, by Moreelse. The two great pictures of the gallery hang opposite each other. That by Bartholomew van der Helst, the most famous of Dutch portrait-painters, represents the Banquet of the Musqueteers, who thus celebrated the Peace of Westphalia, June 18, 1648. It contains twenty-five life-size portraits, is the best work of the master, and was pronounced by Sir Joshua Reynolds to be the 'first picture of portraits in the world.' The canvas is a mirror faithfully representing a scene of actual life. In the centre sits the jovial, rollicking Captain de Wits with his legs crossed. The delicate imitation of reality is equally shown in the Rhenish wine-glasses, and in the ham to which one of the guests is helping himself.

The rival picture is the 'Night Watch' of Rembrandt (1642), representing Captain Frans Banning Kok of Purmerland and his lieutenant Willem van Ruytenberg of Vlaardingen, emerging from their watch-house on the Singel. A joyous troop pursue their leader, who is in a black dress. A strange light comes upon the scene, who can tell whence? Half society has always said that this picture was the marvel of the world, half that it is unworthy of its artist; but no one has ever been quite indifferent to it.

Of the other pictures we must at least notice, by Nicholas Maas, a thoughtful girl leaning on a cushion out of a window with apricots beneath; and by Jan Steen, 'The Parrot Cage,' a simple scene of tavern life, in which the waiting-maid calls to the parrot hanging aloft, who looks knowingly out of the cage, whilst all the other persons present go on with their different employments. In the 'Eve of S. Nicholas,' another work of the same artist, a naughty boy finds a birch-rod in his shoe, and a good little girl, laden with gifts, is being praised by her mother, whilst other children are looking up the chimney by which the discriminating fairy Befana is supposed to have taken her departure. There are many beautiful works of Ruysdael, most at home amongst waterfalls; a noble Vandyke of 'William II.' as a boy, with his little bride, Mary Stuart, Charles I.'s daughter, in a brocaded silver dress; and the famous Terburg called 'Paternal Advice' (known in England by its replica at Bridgewater House), in which a daughter in white satin is receiving a lecture from her father, her back turned to the spectator, and her annoyance, or repentance, only exhibited in her shoulders. Another famous work of Terburg is 'The Letter,' which is being brought in by a trumpeter to an officer seated in his uniform, with his young wife kneeling at his side. Of Gerard Dou Amsterdam possesses the wonderful 'Evening School,' with four luminous candles, and some thoroughly Dutch children. A girl is laboriously following with her finger the instructions received, and a boy is diligently writing on a slate. The girl who stands behind, instructing him, is holding a candle which throws a second light upon his back, that upon the table falling on his features; indeed the painting is often known as the 'Picture of the Four Candles.'

Through the labyrinthine quays we found our way to the Westerhoof to take the afternoon steamer to Purmerende for an excursion to Broek, 'the cleanest village in the world.' Crossing the broad Amstel, the vessel soon enters a canal, which sometimes lies at a great depth, nothing being visible but the tops of masts and points of steeples; and which then, after passing locks, becomes level with the tops of the trees and the roofs of the houses. We left the steamer at T Schouw, and entered, on a side canal, one of the trekschuiten, which, until the time of railroads, were the usual means of travel—a long narrow cabin, encircled by seats, forms the whole vessel, and is drawn by a horse ridden by a boy (het-jagerte)—a most agreeable easy means of locomotion, for movement is absolutely imperceptible.

No place was ever more exaggerated than Broek. There is really very little remarkable in it, except even a greater sense of dampness and ooziness than in the other Dutch villages. It was autumn, and there seemed no particular attempt to remove the decaying vegetation or trim the little gardens, or to sweep up the dead leaves upon the pathways, yet there used to be a law that no animal was to enter Broek for fear of its being polluted. A brick path winds amongst the low wooden cottages, painted blue, green, and white, and ends at the church, with its miniature tombstones.

The most interesting excursion to be made from

Amsterdam is that to the Island of Marken in the Zuider Zee—a huge meadow, where the peasant women pass their whole lives without ever seeing anything beyond their island, whilst their husbands, who with very few exceptions are fishermen, see nothing beyond the fisher-towns of the Zuider Zee. There are very picturesque costumes here, the men wearing red woollen shirts, brown vests, wooden shoes, fur caps, and gold buttons to their collars and knickerbockers ; the women, embroidered stomachers, which are handed down for generations, and enormous white caps, lined with brown to show off the lace, and with a chintz cover for week days, and their own hair flowing below the cap over their shoulders and backs.

An evening train, with an old lady, in a diamond tiara and gold pins, for our companion, took us to the Helder, and we awoke next morning at the pleasant little inn of Du Burg upon a view of boats and nets and the low-lying Island of Texel in the distance. The boats and the fishermen are extremely picturesque, but there is nothing else to see, after the visitor has examined the huge granite Helder Dyke, the artificial fortification of north Holland, which contends successfully to preserve the land against the sea. There is an admirably managed Naval Institute here. It was by an expedition from the Helder that Nova Zembla was discovered, and it was near this that Admirals Ruyter and Tromp repulsed the English fleet. Texel, which lies opposite the Helder, is the first of a chain of islands—Vlieland, Terschelling, and Ameland, which protect the entrance of the Zuider Zee.

The country near the Helder is bare and desolate in the extreme. It is all peat, and the rest of Holland uses it as a fuel mine. It was here that the genius of Ruysdael was often able to make a single tree, or even a bush rising out of the flat by a stagnant pool, both interesting and charming to the spectator. We crossed the levels to Alkmaar, which struck us as being altogether the prettiest place in the country and as possessing all those attributes of cleanliness which are usually given to Brock. The streets, formed of bricks fitted close together, are absolutely spotless, and every house front shines fresh from the mop or the syringe. Yet excessive cleanliness has not destroyed the picturesqueness of the place. The fifteenth-century church of S. Lawrence, of exquisitely graceful exterior, rises in the centre of the town, and, in spite of being hideously defaced inside, has a fine vaulted roof, a coloured screen, and, in the chancel, a curious tomb to Florens V., Count of Holland, 1296, though only his heart is buried there. Near the excellent Hôtel du Burg is a most bewitching almshouse, with an old tourelle and screen, and a lovely garden in a court surrounded by clipped lime-trees. And more charming still is an old weigh-house of 1582, for the cheese, the great manufacture of the district, for which there

APPROACH TO ALKMAAR.

is a famous market every Friday, where capital costumes may be seen. The rich and gaily painted façade of the old building, reflected in a clear canal, is a perfect marvel of beauty and colour; and artists should stay here to paint—not the view given here, but another which we discovered too late—more in front, with gable-ended houses leading up to the principal building, and all its glowing colours repeated in the water.

It is three hours' drive from Alkmaar to Hoorn, a charming old town with bastions, gardens, and

THE WEIGH-HOUSE, ALKMAAR.

semi-ruined gates. On the West Poort a relief commemorates the filial devotion of a poor boy, who arrived here in 1579, laboriously dragging his old mother in a sledge, when all were flying from the

Spaniards. Opposite the weighing-house for the cheeses is the State College, which bears a shield with the arms of England, sustained by two negroes. It commemorates the fact that when Van Tromp defeated the English squadron, his ships came from Hoorn and on board were two negroes, who took from the English flagship the shield which it was then the custom to fix to the stern of a vessel, and brought it back here as a trophy. Hoorn was one of the first places in Holland to embrace the reformed religion, which spread from hence all over the country, but now not above half the inhabitants are Calvinists.

In returning from Alkmaar we stopped to see Zaandam, quite in the centre of the land of windmills, of which we counted eighty as visible from the station alone. They are of every shade of colour, and are mounted on poles, on towers, on farm buildings, and made picturesque by every conceivable variety of prop, balcony, gallery, and insertion. Zaandam is a very pretty village on the Zaan which flows into the Y, with gaily painted houses, and gay little gardens, and perpetual movement to and from its landing-stage. Turning south from thence, a little entry on the right leads down some steps and over a bridge to some cottages on the bank of a ditch, and inside the last of these is the tiny venerable hovel where Peter the

Great stayed in 1697 as Peter Michaeloff. It retains its tiled roof and contains some old chairs and a box-bed, but unfortunately Peter was only here a week.

The evening of leaving Zaandam we spent at Utrecht, of which the name is so well known from

MILL AT ZAANDAM.

the peace which terminated the war of the Spanish succession, April 11, 1715. The town, long the seat of an ecclesiastical court, was also the great centre of the Jansenists, dissenters from Roman Catholicism under Jansenius, Bishop of Ypres, condemned by

Alexander VII. in 1656, at the instigation of the Jesuits. The doctrines of Jansenius still linger in its gloomy houses. Every appointment of a bishop is still announced to the Sovereign Pontiff, who as regu-

PAUSHUIZEN, UTRECHT.

larly responds by a bull of excommunication, which is read aloud in the cathedral, and then immediately put away and forgotten. Solemn and sad, but pre-eminently respectable, Utrecht has more the aspect of a decayed German city than a Dutch town, and so has its Cathedral of S. Martin (1254-67), which, though the finest Gothic building in Holland, is only a magnificent fragment, with a detached tower (1321-82) 338 feet high. The interior as usual is ruined by Calvinism and yellow paint. It contains the tomb of Admiral van Gent, who fell in the battle of Solbay. The nave, which fell in 1674, has never been rebuilt. The S. Pieterskerk (1039) and S. Janskerk offer nothing remarkable, but on a neighbouring canal is the quaint Paushuizen, or Pope's house, which was built by Pope Adrian VI. (Adrian Floriszoom) in 1517. Near this is the pretty little Archiepiscopal Museum, full of mediæval relics.

The interesting Moravian establishment of Zeist may be visited from Utrecht.

From Utrecht we travelled over sandy flats to Kampen, near the mouth of the wide river Yssel, with three picturesque gates— Haghen Poort, Cellebroeders Poort, and Broeders Poort; and a town hall of the sixteenth century. Here, as frequently elsewhere in Holland, we suffered from arriving famished at midday. All the inns were equally inhospitable: 'The table d'hote is at 4 P.M.: we *cannot* and *will not* be bothered with cooking before that, and there is nothing cold in the house.' 'But you have surely bread and cheese?' 'Certainly not—*nothing*.'

At Zwolle, however, we found the Kroon an excellent hotel with an obliging landlord; and Zwolle, the native place of Terburg (1608), is a charming old

CELLEBROEDERS POORT, KAMPEN.

town with a girdle of gardens, a fine church (externally), and a noble brick gateway called the Sassenpoort.

It was more the desire of seeing something of the

whole country than anything else, and a certain degree of misplaced confidence in the pleasant volumes of Harvard, which took us up from Zwolle, through

SASSENPOORT, AT ZWOLLE.

Friesland, the cow-paradise, to Leeuwarden, its ancient capital. Sad and gloomy as most other towns of Holland are, Leeuwarden is sadder and gloomier still. Its streets are wide and not otherwise than handsome, but they are almost deserted, and there are no objects of interest to see unless a leaning tower can be called so, with a top, like that at Pisa, inclined the other way, to keep it from toppling over. An hour's walk from the town there is said to be a fine still-inhabited castle, and, if time had allowed, respect for S. Boniface would have taken us to Murmerwoude, where he was martyred (June 8, 853), with his fifty-three companions. King Pepin raised a hermitage on the spot, and an ancient brick chapel still exists there.

Here and elsewhere in Friesland nothing is so worthy of notice as the helmets — the golden helmets of the women—costing something equivalent to 25*l.* or 30*l.*, handed down as heirlooms, fitting close to the head, and not allowing a particle of hair to be visible.

In the late evening we went on to Groningen, a university town with a good hotel (Seven Provincen), an enormous square, and a noble tall Gothic tower of 1627, whence the watchman still sounds his bugle. Not far off is Midwolde, where the village church has fine tombs of Charles Jerome, Baron d'Inhausen and his wife, Anna von Ewsum.

As late as the sixteenth century this province was for the most part uninhabited—savage and sandy, and overrun by wolves. But three hundred years of hard work has transformed it into a fertile country, watered by canals, and sprinkled with country houses. Agriculturally it is one of the richest provinces of the kingdom. This is mostly due to its possessing a race of peasant-farmers who never shrink from personal hard work, and who will continue to direct the plough whilst they send their sons to the university to study as lawyers, doctors, or churchmen. These peasant farmers or boers possess the *beklemregt*, or right of hiring land on an annual rent, which the landlord can never increase. A peasant can bequeath his right to his heirs, whether direct or collateral. To the land, this system is an indescribable advantage, the cultivators doing their utmost to bring their lands to perfection, because they are certain that no one can take away the advantage from themselves or their descendants.

On leaving Groningen we traversed the grey, monotonous, desolate district of the Drenthe, sprinkled over at intervals by the curious ancient groups of stones called Hunnebedden, or beds of death (Hun meaning death), beneath which urns of clay containing human ashes have been found. From Deventer (where there is an old weigh-house, and a cathedral of S. Lievin with a crypt and nave of 1334), time did not allow us to make an excursion to the great royal palace of Het Loo, the favourite residence of the sovereigns. The descriptions in Harvard rather made us linger unnecessarily at Zutphen, a dull town, with a brick Groote Kerk (S. Walpurgis) which has little remaining of its original twelfth-century date, and a rather picturesque 'bit' on the walls, where the 'Waterpoort' crosses the river like a bridge.

At Arnhem, the Roman Arenacum, once the residence of the Dukes of Gueldres, and still the capital of Guelderland, we seemed to have left all the characteristics of Holland behind. Numerous modern villas, which might have been built for Cheltenham or Leamington, cover the wooded hills above the Rhine. In the Groote Kerk (1452) is a curious monument of Charles van Egmont, Duc de Gueldres, 1538, but there is nothing else to remark upon. We intended to have made an excursion hence to Cleves, but desperately wet weather set in, and, as Dutch rain often lasts for weeks together when it once begins, we were glad to hurry England-wards, only regretting that we could not halt at Nymegen, a most picturesque place, where Charlemagne lived in the old palace of the Valckhof (or Waalhof, residence on the Waal), of which a fragment still exists, with an old baptistery, a Stadhuis of 1534, and a Groote Kerk containing a noble monument to Catherine de Bourbon (1469), wife of Duke Adolph of Gueldres.

We left Holland feeling that we should urge our friends by all means to see the pictures at Rotterdam, the Hague, and Amsterdam, but to look for all other characteristics of the Netherlands in such places as Breda, Dortrecht, Haarlem, Alkmaar, and Zwolle.

IN DENMARK

IN DENMARK.

FORMERLY the terrors of a sea-voyage from Kiel deterred many travellers from thinking of a tour in Denmark or Sweden, but now a succession of railways makes everything easy, and while nothing can be imagined more invigorating or pleasant, there is probably no pleasure more economical than a summer in Scandinavia. Those who are worn with a London season will feel as if every breath in the crystal air of Denmark endued them with fresh health and strength, and then, after they have seen its old palaces and its beech woods and its Thorwaldsen sculptures, a voyage of ten minutes will carry them over the narrow Sound to the soft beauties of genial Sweden and the wild splendours of Norway.

Either Hamburg or Lübeck must be the starting-point for the overland route to Denmark, and the old free city of Lübeck, though quite a small place, is one of the most remarkable towns in Germany. We arrived there one hot summer afternoon, after a weary journey over the arid sandy plains which separate it from Berlin, and suddenly seemed to be transported into a land of verdure. Lilacs and roses bloomed everywhere; a wood lined the bank of the limpid river Trave, and in its waters—beyond the old wooden bridge—were reflected all the tallest steeples, often strangely out of the perpendicular, of many-towered Lübeck. A wonderful gate of red brick and golden-hued terra-cotta is the entrance from the station, and in the market-place are the quaintest turrets, towers, tourelles, but all ending in spires. The lofty houses, so full of rich colour, throw cool shade on the streets on the hottest summer day; and we enjoyed a Sunday in the excellent hotel, with wooden galleries opening towards a splashing fountain in a quiet square, where a fat constable busied himself in keeping everybody from fulfilling any avocation whatever whilst service was being performed in the churches, but let them do exactly as they pleased as soon as it was over.

It must, at best, be a weary journey across West Holstein, through a succession of arid flats varied by stagnant swamps. We spent the weary hours in studying Dunham's 'History of Denmark, Sweden, and Norway,' which cannot be sufficiently recommended to all Scandinavian travellers. The glowing accounts in the English guide books of a lake and an old castle beguiled us into spending a night at Sleswig, but it turned out that the lake had disappeared before the memory of man, and that the castle was a white modern barrack. The colourless town and its long sleepy suburb, moored as if upon a raft in the marshes, straggle along the edge of a waveless fiord. At the end is the rugged cathedral like a barn, with a belfry like a dovecot, and inside it a curious altarpiece by Hans Brüggemann, pupil of Albert Dürer, and the noble monument of Frederick I., the first Lutheran King of Denmark; while richly carved doors at the sides of the church admit one to see how the grandmother of the Princess of Wales and various other potentates lie—Danish fashion—in gorgeous exposed coffins without any tombs at all. Everywhere roses grow in the streets, trained upon the house walls; and, up the pavement, crowds of the children were hurrying in the early morning, carrying in their hands the shoes they were going to wear when they were in school. In the evenings these children will not venture outside the town, for over the marshes they say that the wild huntsman rides, followed by his demon hounds and blowing his magic horn. It is the spirit of Duke Abel the fratricide, who, in the fens, murdered his brother Eric VI. of Denmark, and who was afterwards lost there himself, falling from his horse, and being dragged down by the weight of his armour. To give rest to his wandering spirit, the clergy dug up his body and despatched it to Bremen, but there his vampire gave the canons no peace, so they sent the corpse back again, and now it lies once more in the marshes of Gottorp.

Most unutterably hideous is the country through which the railway now travels, wearisome levels only broken here and there by mounds, probably sepulchral. A straight line with tiny hillocks at intervals would do for a sketch of the whole of Sleswig and the greater part of Funen and Zealand. In times of early Danish history it was a frequent punishment to bury criminals alive in these dismal peat mosses. Twelve hours of changelessly flat scenery bring travellers from Hamburg to Frederikshaven, where we embark upon the Little Belt, the luggage-vans of the train being shunted on board the steamer. Immediately opposite lie the sandy shores of Funen, and in a few minutes we are there. Then four hours of ugly scenery take us across the island. It is only necessary to look out at the little town of Odense, called after the old hero-god, which was the birthplace of Hans Christian Andersen in 1805. The cathedral of Odense contains the shrine of the sainted

King Canute IV. (1080-86), who was murdered while kneeling before the altar, owing to indignation at the severe taxation to which the love of Church endowment had incited him.

Nyborg, where we meet the sea again, will recall to lovers of old ballads the story of the innocent young knight Folker Lowmanson, and his cruel death here in a barrel of spikes, from the jealousy of Waldemar IV. for his beautiful queen Helwig, and how, to know his fate—

> With anxious heart did Denmark's Queen
>   To Nyborg urge her horse,
> And at the gate his bier she met,
>   And on it Folker's corse.
>
> Such honour shown to son of knight
>   I never yet could hear;
> The Queen of Denmark walked on foot
>   Herself before his bier.
>
> In tears then Helwig mounted horse
>   And silent homeward rode,
> For in her heart a life-long grief
>   Had taken its abode.

At Nyborg we embark on a miserable steamer for the passage of the Great Belt. It lasts an hour and a half, and is often most wretched. On landing at Korsor travellers are hurried into the train which is waiting for the vessel.

F

Now the country improves a little. Here and there we pass through great beech woods. Down the green glades of one of them a glimpse is caught of the college of Sorö. It occupies the site of a monastery founded by Asker Ryg, a chieftain who, when he departed on a journey of warfare, vowed that if the child to which his wife, Inge, was about to give birth proved to be a girl, he would give his new building a spire, but a tower if it were a boy. On his return he saw two towers rising in the distance. Inge had given birth to twin sons, who lived to become Asbiorn Snare, celebrated in the ballad of 'Fair Christal,' and Absalon, the warrior Bishop of Roeskilde—'first captain by sea and land.' Absalon is buried here in the church of Sorö, which contains the tomb of King Olaf, the shortlived son of the famous Queen Margaret; of her cruel father, Waldemar Atterdag, whose last words expressed regret that he had not suffocated his daughter in her cradle; and of her grandfather, Christopher II., with his wife, Euphemia of Pomerania. Soon we pass Ringsted, which is scarcely worth stopping at, though its church contains the fine brass of King Erik Menred (1319) and his queen, Ingeborga, and though twenty kings and queens were entombed there before Roeskilde became the royal place of sepulture. Amongst them lies the popular Queen Dagmar, first wife of Waldemar II., still celebrated in ballad literature, for there is scarcely a Dane who is ignorant of the touching story of 'Queen Dagmar's Death,' which begins

> Queen Dagmar is lying at Ribé sick,
> At Ringsted is made her grave,

and which contains her last touching request to her husband, and her simple confession of the only 'sin' she could remember—

> Had I on a Sunday not laced my sleeves,
> Or border upon them sewn,
> No pangs had I felt by day or night,
> Or torture of hell-fire known.

Tradition tells us that the dismal town of Ringsted was founded by King Ring, a warrior who, when he was seriously wounded in battle, placed the bodies of his slain heroes and that of his queen, Alpol, on board a ship laden with pitch, and going out to the open sea, set the vessel on fire, and then fell upon his sword.

In the twilight we pass Roeskilde, and at 10½ P.M. long rows of street lamps reflected in canals show that we have reached Copenhagen.

To those whose travels have chiefly led them southwards there is a great pleasure in the first awaking in Copenhagen. Everything is new—the associations, the characteristics, the history ; even the very names on the omnibuses are suggestive of the sagas and romances of the North ; and though the summer sun is hot, the atmosphere is as clear as that of a tramontana day in an Italian winter, and the air is indescribably elastic. The comfortable Hôtel d'Angleterre stands in the Kongens Nytorv, a modern square, with trees surrounding a statue in the centre, but there are glimpses of picturesque shipping down the side streets, and hard by is a spire quite ideally Danish, formed by three marvellous dragons with their tails twisted together in the air. Tradition declares that it was moved bodily from Calmar, in the south of Sweden. It rises now from a beautiful building of brick erected in 1624 by Christian IV., brother-in-law of James I. of England, and used as the Exchange.

Not far off is the principal palace—Christiansborg Slot, often rebuilt, and very white and ugly. It was partially destroyed by fire in 1884. Besides the royal residence, its vast courts contain the Chambers of Parliament, the Royal Library, and a Picture Gallery chiefly filled with the works of native artists, amongst which those of Marstrand and Bloch are very striking and well worthy of attention.

A queer building in the shadow of the palace,

COPENHAGEN. 69

which attracts notice by its frescoed walls, is the Thorwaldsen Museum, the shrine where Denmark has reverentially collected all the works and memorials of her greatest artist—Bertel Thorwaldsen. Though

THE DRAGON TOWER, COPENHAGEN.

his family is said to have descended from the Danish king Harold Stildetand, he was born (in 1770) the son of one Gottschalk, who, half workman, half artist, was employed in carving figures for the bows of vessels.

From his earliest childhood little Bertel accompanied his father to the wharfs and assisted him in his work, in which he showed such intelligence that in his eleventh year he was allowed to enter the Free School of Art. Here he soon made wonderful progress in sculpture, but could so little be persuaded to attend to other studies that he reached the age of eighteen scarcely able to read. In his twenty-third year he obtained the great gold medal, to which a travelling stipend is attached, and thus he was enabled to go to Rome, where, encouraged at first by the patronage of Thomas Hope, the English banker, he soon reached the highest pitch of celebrity. Denmark became proud of her son, so that his visits to his native town in 1819 and 1837 were like triumphal progresses, all the city going forth to meet him, and lodging him splendidly at the public cost; but his heart always clung to the Eternal City, which continued to be the scene of his labours. Of his many works perhaps his noble lion at Lucerne is the best known. He never married, though he was long attached to a member of the old Scottish house of Mackenzie, and he died on a visit to Copenhagen in 1844.

In accordance with Thorwaldsen's own wish, he rests in the centre of his works. His grave has no tombstone, but is covered with green ivy. All around the little court which contains it are halls and galleries filled with the marvellously varied productions of his genius, arranged in the order of their execution—casts of all his absent sculptures and many most grand originals. Especially beautiful are the statue of Mercury, modelled from a Roman boy, of which the original is in the possession of Lord Ashburton, and the exquisite reliefs of the Ages of Love, and of Day and Night, the two latter resulting from the inspiration of a single afternoon. But all seem to culminate in the great Hall of Christ, for though the statues here are only cast from those in the Vor Frue Kirche, they are far better seen in the well-lighted chamber than in the church. The colossal figures of the apostles lead up to the Saviour in sublime benediction; perhaps the statues of Simon Zelotes and the pilgrim S. James are the noblest amongst them. In the last room are gathered all the little personal memorials of Thorwaldsen—his books, pictures, and furniture.

The Museum of Northern Antiquities should also be visited and the Tower of the Trinity Church, with a roadway inside making an easy ascent to the strange view of many roofs and many waters which is obtained from the top. But the most delightful place in Copenhagen is the Palace of Rosenborg, standing at the end of a stately old garden—where it was built by Inigo

Jones for Christian IV., and containing the room where the king died, with his wedding dress, and most of his other clothes and possessions. This palace-building monarch, celebrated for the drinking bouts in which

THE ROSENBORG PALACE, COPENHAGEN.

he indulged with his brother-in-law, James I. of England, was the greatest dandy of his time, and before we leave Denmark we shall become very familiar with his portraits, always distinguished by the wonderful left whisker twisted into a pigtail falling on one side of the chin. Other rooms in Rosenborg are devoted to each of the succeeding sovereigns, and filled with relics and memorials which carry one back into most romantic corners of Danish history, the ever-alternate succession of Christians and Fredericks making a most terrible bewilderment, down to the two English queens, Louisa the beloved and Caroline Matilda the unfortunate. Most curious amongst a myriad objects of value are the three great silver Lions—'Great Belt, Little Belt, and Sound'—which, by ancient custom, appear as mourners at all the funerals of the sovereigns, accompanying them to Roeskilde and returning afterwards to the palace.

Those interested in such matters will wander as we did through the more ancient parts of Copenhagen in search of old silver and specimens of the older Copenhagen china. Formerly the china imitated that of Miessen, but it has now a more distinctive character, and is chiefly used in reproducing the works of Thorwaldsen. Copenhagen has no other especial manufactures.

No visitors to the Danish capital must omit a visit to Tivoli, the pretty odd pleasure grounds—very respectable too—near the railway station, where all kinds of evening amusements are provided in illuminated gardens and woods by a tiny lake, really very pretty. Here we watched the cars rushing like a whirlwind down one hill and up another, with their inmates screaming in pleasurable agony; and saw the extraordinary feats of 'the Cannon King,' who tossed a cannon ball, catching it on his hands, his head, his feet—anywhere, and then stood in front of a cannon and was shot, receiving in his hands the ball, which did nothing worse than twist him round by its force.

One day we went out—an hour and a half by rail —to Roeskilde, where a church was first founded by William, an Englishman, in the days of King Harold Blaatand (Blue-tooth), brother of Canute the Great. It is dedicated to S. Lucius, because tradition tells that a terrible dragon, who infested the neighbouring fiord and banqueted on the inhabitants, was destroyed for ever when the head of the holy Pope S. Lucius was brought from Rome and presented for his breakfast. The tall spires of the cathedral rise, slender and grey, from the little town, and beneath, embosomed in sweeping cornfields, a lovely fiord stretches away into pale blue distances. Endless kings and queens are buried at Roeskilde. The earlier sovereigns have glorious tombs, amongst which the most conspicuous is that of Queen Margaret—'the Semiramis of the North,' who, born in the prison of Syborg, where her unhappy mother Queen Helwig was imprisoned by Waldemar Atterhag, and allowed to run wild in the forest in her childhood, lived to become one of the wisest of Northern sovereigns, and to unite, by the Act known as 'the Union of Calmar,' the crowns of Denmark, Sweden, and Norway, which attained unwonted

ROESKILDE.

prosperity under her sway. There are effigies of Frederic II. and Christian IV., the grandfather and uncle of our Charles I., which recall his type of countenance and have the same peaked beard. Christian IV., the great palace-builder, whose birth was believed to have been prophesied by the mermaid Isbrand, was born (April 12, 1577) under a hawthorn tree on the road between Frederiksborg and Roeskilde, as his mother, Sophia of Mecklenbourg, insisted on taking walks with her ladies in waiting far longer than was prudent. This king, his father, and all the later members of his royal house lie, not in their tombs, but in gorgeous coffins embossed with gold and silver upon the floor of the church, which has a very odd effect. The entrance of one of the private chapels is a gate with a huge figure, in wrought ironwork, of the devil with his tail in his hand. In another chapel are fine works of Marstrand (1810-75), the best of the pupils of Eckersberg, who gave the first stimulus to the art of painting in Denmark, where it has since attained to great eminence.

The district around Roeskilde, and indeed the greater part of Denmark, is devoted to corn, for there is no country in Europe, except England and Belgium, which can compete with this as a corn-grower. It is curious that though the neighbouring Sweden and Norway are so covered with pines, no conifer will grow in Denmark except under most careful cultivation. The principal native tree is the beech, and the beech woods are nowhere more beautiful than in the neighbourhood of Copenhagen. The railway to Elsinore passes through the beautiful beech forests which are familiar to us through the stories of Hans

Christian Andersen. Here, near a little roadside station, rises the Hampton Court of Denmark, the great Castle of Frederiksborg, the most magnificent of the creations of Christian IV., which John of Friburg erected for that monarch, who looked personally into the minutest details of his expenses, and

THE CASTLE OF FREDERIKSBORG.

so raised this structure, glorious as it is, with an economy which greatly astonished his thrifty parliament. In the depths of the beech woods is a great lake, in the centre of which, on three islands united by bridges, rises the palace, most beautiful in its time-honoured hues of red brick and grey stone, with high roofs, richly sculptured windows, and wondrous towers and spires. Each view of the castle seems more picturesque than the last. It is a dream of architectural beauty, to which the great expanse of transparent waters and the deep verdure of the surrounding woods add a mysterious charm. A gigantic gate tower admits the visitor to the courtyard, where Christian IV., with his own hand, chopped off the head of the Master of the Mint, which he had established here, who had defrauded him. 'He tried to cheat us, but we have cheated him, for we have chopped his head off,' said the King. Inside, the palace has been gorgeously restored since a great fire by which it was terribly injured in 1859. The chapel, with the pew of Christian IV.—'bedekammer,' prayer chamber, it is called—is most curious. There is a noble series of the pictures of the native artist Carl Bloch, recalling the works of Overbeck in their majesty and depth of feeling, but far more forcible.

A drive of four miles through beech woods leads to the comfortable later palace of Fredensborg, built as 'a Castle of Peace' by Frederick IV. and Louisa of Mecklenbourg, with a lovely garden, and a view of the Esrom lake down green glades, in one of which is a mysterious assembly of stone statues in Norwegian costumes.

We may either take the railway or drive by Gurre from hence to Elsinore (Helsingor), where the great castle of Kronberg rises, with many towers built of grey stone, at the end of the little town on a low promontory jutting out into the sea. Stately avenues surround its bastions, and it is delightful to walk upon the platform where the first scene of Shakspere's 'Hamlet' is laid, and to watch the numberless ships in

CASTLE OF ELSINORE.

the narrow Sound which divides Denmark and Sweden. The castle is in perfect preservation. It was formerly used as a palace. Anne of Denmark was married here by proxy to James VI. of Scotland, and here poor Caroline Matilda sate daily for hours at her prison window watching vainly for the fleet of England which she believed was coming to her rescue. Beyond the castle, a sandy plain reminding us of Scottish links, covered with bent-grass and drifted by seaweed, extends to Marienlyst, a little fashionable bathing place embosomed in verdure. Here a Carmelite convent was founded by the wife of Eric IX., that Queen Philippa—daughter of Henry IV. of England—who successfully defended Copenhagen against the Hanseatic League, but was afterwards beaten by her husband, because her ships were defeated at Stralsund, an indignity which drove her to a monastic life. Hamlet's Grave and Ophelia's Brook are shown at Marienlyst, having been invented for anxious inquirers by the complaisant inhabitants. Alas! both were unknown to Andersen, who lived here in his childhood, and it is provoking to learn that Hamlet had really no especial connection with Elsinore, and was the son of a Jutland pirate in the insignificant island of Mors. But Denmark is the very home of picturesque stories, which are kept alive there by the ballad literature of the land, chiefly of the fourteenth or fifteenth centuries, but still known to rich and poor alike as in no other country. For hundreds of years these poetical histories have been the tunes to which, in winter, when no other exercise can be taken, people dance for hours, holding each other's hands in two lines, making three steps forwards and backwards, keeping time, balancing, or remaining still for a moment, as they sing one of their old ballads or its refrain.

TOWER OF HELSINGBORG CHURCH.

It was in a wild evening, with huge blue foam-crested waves rushing down the Sound, that we crossed in ten minutes to Helsingborg in Sweden, mounted for the sunset to the one huge remaining tower of its castle, and sketched as typical of almost all village towers in Denmark the belfry of the church where King Eric Menred was married to the Swedish princess Ingeborga.

IN SWEDEN

IN SWEDEN.

IT is not beautiful in Sweden, but it is very pretty; if everything were not so very much alike, it would be very pretty indeed. The whole country as far north as Upsala is like an exaggerated Surrey—little hills covered with fir-woods and bilberries, brilliant, glistening little lakes sleeping in sandy hollows, but all just like one another.

We turned aside in our way from Helsingborg to the north to visit the old university of Lund, the Oxford of Sweden, a sleepy city, where the students lead a separate life in lodgings of their own, only being united in the public lectures; for in Sweden, as in Italy, the taking of a degree only proves that the graduates have passed a certain number of examinations, not, as in England, that they have lived together for three years at least, forming their character and taste by mutual companionship and intimacy. The cathedral of Lund is a most noble Norman building, with giants and dwarfs sculptured against the pillars of its grand crypt, and a glorious archbishop's tomb, green and mossy with damp.

An immense railway journey, by day and night through the endless forests, brought us to Stockholm, where we arrived in the early morning. Though the town is little beyond an ugly collection of featureless modern streets, the situation is quite exquisite, for the

THE JUNCTION OF LAKE MALAR AND THE BALTIC, STOCKHOLM.

city occupies a succession of islets between Lake Malar and the Baltic, surrounding, on a central isle, the huge Palace built from stately designs of Count Tessin in the middle of the last century, and the old church of Riddarholmen, where Gustavus Adolphus and many other royal persons repose beneath the banner-hung arches.

It sounds odd, but, next to the Palace, the most imposing building in Stockholm is certainly the Grand Hotel Rydberg, which is most comfortable and economical, in spite of its palatial aspect. There is no table d'hôte, and everything is paid for at the time, in the excellent restaurant on the first floor of the hotel. Here, a side table is always covered with dainties peculiarly Swedish, corn and birch brandy, and different kinds of potted fish, with fresh butter and olives, and it is the universal custom in Sweden to attack the side table before sitting down to the regular dinner. The rooms in the hotel are excellent, and their front windows overlook all that is most characteristic in Stockholm—the glorious view down the fiord of the Baltic: its farther hilly bank covered with houses and churches; the bridge at the junction of the Baltic and Lake Malar, which is the centre of life in the capital, and the little pleasure garden below, where hundreds of people are constantly eating and drinking under the trees, and whence strains of music are wafted late into the summer night; the mighty palace dominating the principal island, and the little steam gondolas, filled with people, which dart and hiss through the waters from one island to another. In Stockholm, where waters are many and bridges few, these steam gondolas are the chief means of communication, and we made great use of them, the passages costing twelve oëre, or one penny. The great white sea-gulls, poising over the water-streets or floating upon the waves, are also a striking feature.

The museums of Stockholm have little to call for any especial notice, except a grand statue of the sleeping Endymion from the Villa Adriana, and the curious collection of royal clothes down to the present date, a gallery of costume like that which once existed in London at the Tower Royal. The chief curiosity which the Swedish collection contains is the hat worn by Charles XII. when he was killed, in which the upward progress of the bullet can be traced, proving that the king's death was caused by an assassin, and not the result of a chance shot from the walls of Frederikshald. No especial features mark the interior of the Palace, though the Royal Stable for a hundred and forty-six horses is worthy of a visit; and the churches are uninteresting, except perhaps S. Nicholas, the coronation church, which contains the helmet and spurs of S. Olaf, stolen from Throndtjem. Riddarholmen can scarcely be regarded as a church : it is rather a great sepulchral hall hung with trophies, having a few tombs on the floor of the building, and vaults opening under the side walls, in which the different groups of royal persons are buried together in families. Under a chapel on the left lies Gustavus Adolphus, the justly popular great-grandson of Gustavus Wasa, who fell at the battle of Lutzen, and who, as soldier, general, and king, ever knew true merit, and laboured for the glory of his country rather than for his own. In the opposite chapel repose the present royal family, descendants of Bernadotte, Prince of Pontecorvo, the only one of Napoleon's generals whose dynasty still, occupies a throne. He began life as a common soldier, and his election as Charles XIV. of Sweden was chiefly due to the kindness with which he treated Swedish prisoners taken in the Pomeranian wars. But the Swedes have never had cause to repent of their choice, and their reigning house is probably the most popular in Europe. The coffins of those members of the royal family who have died within the memory of man are ever laden with fresh flowers.

Close by the Riddarholmen Church is the most picturesque bit of street architecture in Stockholm, where a statue of Burger Jarl, the traditional founder of the town, forms a foreground to the chapel of Gustavus Adolphus and one of the many bridges.

In saying that Stockholm is not picturesque one

may seem to have spoken disparagingly, but, nevertheless, it is perfectly charming: there is so much life and movement upon its blue waters, and its many little public gardens give such a gay aspect to the buildings. Of these, the chief is the Kongsträgården,

RIDDARHOLMEN, STOCKHOLM.

surrounding a statue of Charles XIII., where the pleasant Café Blanche is filled all the evening with an animated crowd, gossiping and eating ices under the verandah and shrubberies, and listening to the music. While we were staying in Stockholm a hundred Upsala students came in their white caps to sing national melodies in the Catherina Church. We lived through two hours of fearful heat to hear them, and most beautiful it was. King Oscar II. was present —a noble royal figure and handsome face. He is the ideal sovereign of the age—artist, poet, musician, student, equally at home in ancient and modern languages, profoundly versed in all his duties, and nobly performing them.

We had intended going often, as the natives do, to dine amongst the trees and flowers at Hasselbacken, in the Djurgården, a wooded promontory, to which little steamers are always plying, but, alas! during eight of the ten July days we spent at Stockholm it rained incessantly. We were so cold that we were thankful for all the winter clothes we brought with us, and were filled with pity for the poor Swedes in being cheated out of their short summer, of which every day is precious. The streets were always sopping, but, in the covered gondolas, we managed several excursions to quiet, damp palaces on the banks of lonely fiords—Rosendal, remarkable for a grand porphyry vase in a brilliant little flower garden; and Ulriksdal, with its clipped avenues and melancholy creek.

Our limited knowledge of Swedish often caused us to embark in amusing ignorance as to whither we were going, and led us into many a surprise. One day we set off, intending to go to Drottningholm, but, on reaching the quay, found the steamer just gone. At that moment such a fearful storm of rain came on that we were obliged to rush for shelter wherever we could, and the nearest point of refuge was the deck of the steamer *Mary*, which instantly started. We feared we might be bound for the Baltic, and, failing to make any one understand us, resolved to disembark at the first landing-place. But then the rain was worse than ever, and we allowed ourselves to be carried on down Lake Malar, till our boat turned into a little creek, and landed us on the pier of a manufacturing town. We had not reached the end of the pier, however, before the rain came on again in such convulsive torrents that we fled back to the *Mary*, which again started on its travels, and this time, after stopping at many little ports, conveyed us back to Stockholm. When we asked the captain what we were to pay for our voyage, he said, 'Oh, nothing;' and very much amused he and his crew seemed to be by our ignorance and adventures.

We had a fine day for our excursion by railway to Upsala, whence we hired a little carriage to take us on to Old Upsala, about three miles distant. A drive across a dull, marshy plain brings one to a delightfully wild district of downs, covered with hundreds of little sepulchral mounds like Wiltshire barrows, amid which three great tumuli, standing close together, are said to mark the graves of Odin, Thor, and Freya—heroes in their lifetime, gods in their death. Close beside them for centuries rose the temple which was the most sacred shrine of Scandinavian worship. It glittered all over with gold, and a golden chain, nine hundred ells in circumference, ran round its roof. In the temple were three statues, around which hovered all the principal mythological traditions of the north. The central figure was that of Odin or Wodan, the wizard-king, who is said to have come in the dawn of Swedish history from his domains of Asir, which extended from the Euxine to the Caspian, and whose capital was Asgard. He landed in Funen, where he founded Odense, and left his son Skjöld as a sovereign. Thence he passed into Sweden, and established his government at Sigtuna, not far from Upsala. His existence is affirmed by the Saxon Chronicle. He was called 'the Father of Victory,' for if he laid his hands on the heads of his generals, and predicted their success when they went out to battle, that success never failed them. He was also, says Snorro Sturlesen, 'the Father of all the arts of modern Europe.' Tradition has endowed him with every miraculous power. He could change his looks at pleasure—to his friends most beautiful, but a demon to his enemies. By his eloquence he captivated all who heard him, and as he always spoke in verse he was called 'the Artificer of Song.' His verses were endowed with such magic power that they could strike his enemies with blindness or deafness, or could blunt their weapons. To listen to the sweetness of his music even the ghosts would come forth and the mountains would unfold their inmost recesses. He was the inventor of Runic characters. He could slaughter thousands at a blow, and he could render his own followers invulnerable. At his will he could assume the form of beasts; at his word the fire would cease to burn, the wind to blow, or the sea to rage. If he hurled his spear between two armies, it secured victory to those on whose side it fell. The dwarfs (Lapps) had built for him a ship called *Skidbladner*, in which he could cross the most dangerous seas with safety; but when he did not want to use it, he could fold it up like a handkerchief. Everything was known to Odin, for did he not possess the mummified head of his enemy Mimir, which was all-wise, and he had only to consult it? Yet, with all these gifts and attributes, Odin remained human; he had no power over death. When he felt his end approaching he assembled all his friends and followers, and, giving himself nine wounds in a circle, allowed himself to bleed to death. The body of the great chieftain was burnt, and his ashes were buried under the mound of Upsala; but his spirit was believed to have gone back to the marvellous home in the Valhalla of Asgard, of which he had so often spoken, and whither he had always said that he should return. Henceforward it

THE GRAVES OF THE GODS.

was considered that all blessings and mercies were gifts sent by Odin. The younger Edda tells that all who die in battle are Odin's adopted children. The Valkyriae pick them out upon the battle-field and conduct them to the Valhalla, where they have perpetual life in the halls of Odin. Their days are spent in hunting or the joys of imaginary combats, and they

return at night to feast upon the inexhaustible flesh of
the boar Sahrimnir, and to drink, out of horn cups, the
mead formed from the milk of a single goat, which is
strong enough nightly to intoxicate all the heroes.
Huge logs constantly burn within the palace of Odin,
for warmth is the northern idea of heaven, while in
their hell it is eternal winter. When a Scandinavian
chieftain died in battle, not only were his war-horse
and all his gold and silver placed upon his funeral-
pyre, but all his followers slew themselves that he
might enter the halls of Odin properly attended.
The more glorious the chieftain the greater the number who must accompany him to Valhalla. To rejoin
Odin in Asgard became the height of a warrior's
ambition. It is recorded of Ragnar Lodbrok that
when he was dying no word of lamentation was
heard from him: on the contrary, he was transported
with joy as he thought of the feast preparing for him
in Odin's palace. 'Soon, soon,' he exclaimed, 'I
shall be seated in the pleasant habitation of the gods,
and drinking mead out of carved horns! A brave
man does not dread death, and I shall utter no word
of fear as I enter the halls of Odin.' But stranger
than all the legends concerning Odin is the fact that
his memory is still so far fresh that 'Go to Odin'
is yet used by the common people where an uncivil

wish as to the lower regions would find expression in England. The fourth day of the week still commemorates Odin or Wodan—in old Norse Odinsdgr, in Swedish and Danish Onsdag, in English Wednesday.

On the right hand of Odin, in the temple of Upsala, sate the statue of Freyja, or Freyer, represented as a hermaphrodite, with the attributes of productiveness. Freyja was the goddess of love, who rode in a car drawn by wild cats. She knew beforehand all that would happen, and divided the souls of the dead with Odin. She is commemorated in the sixth day of the week, that Freytag or Freyja's Day which in Latin is Dies Veneris, or Venus' Day.

On the left of Odin sate Thor, who, says the Edda, was 'the most valiant of the sons of Odin.' He was the offspring of Odin and Frigga, 'the mother of the gods,' and the brother of 'Balder the Beautiful.' As the defender and avenger of the gods, he was represented as carrying the hammer with which he destroyed the giants, and which always returned to his hand when he threw it. He wore iron gauntlets, and had a girdle which doubled his strength when he put it on. The fifth day of the week was sacred to Thor, in old Norse Thórsdag, in Swedish and Danish Torsdag, in English Thursday; in Latin Dies Jovis, for

Jupiter, the God of Thunder, had the same attributes as Thor.

There were three great festivals at Upsala, when multitudes flocked to the temple to consult its famous oracles or to sacrifice. The first was the winter festival of 'Mother Night'—saturnalia in honour of Frey, or the sun, to invoke the blessings of a fruitful year; the second feast was in honour of the Earth; the third was in honour of Odin, to propitiate the Father of Battles. Every ninth year, at least, the king and all persons of distinction were expected to appear before the great temple, and nine victims were chosen for human sacrifice—captives in time of war, slaves in time of peace—'I send thee to Odin' being the consolatory last words spoken to each as he fell. If public calamities had been caused by any royal mismanagement, the people chose their king as a sacrifice; thus the first king of the petty province of Vermeland was burnt to appease Odin during a famine. It is also recorded that King Aun sacrificed his nine sons to obtain a prolongation of his own life. The victims were either hewn down or burnt in the temple itself, or hung in the grove adjoining—'Odin's Grove'—of which every leaf was sacred. Still, according to the Voluspa, the famous prophecy of Vela, at the end of the world even Odin, with all the other pagan deities, will perish in the general chaos, when a new earth of celestial beauty will arise upon the ruins of the old.

One of the most curious little churches in Christendom now stands upon the site of the ancient temple. The apse is evidently built out of the pagan

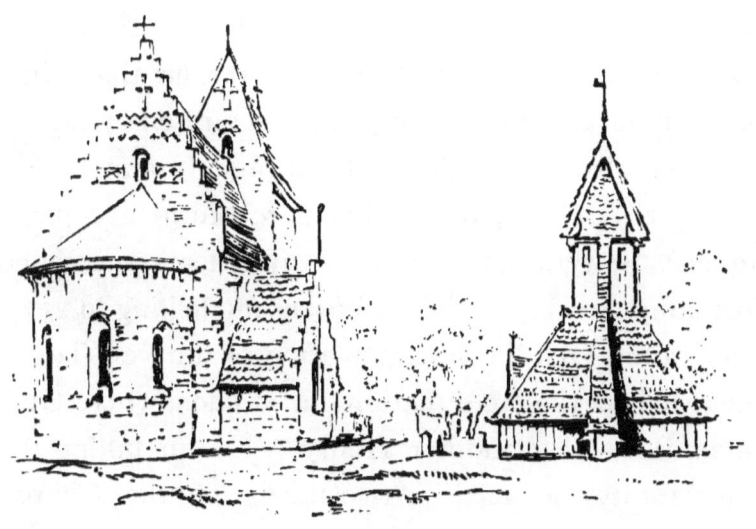

THE CHURCH OF OLD UPSALA.

sanctuary. The belfry, Swedish-fashion, is detached, built of massive timbers and painted bright red. There are scarcely any human habitations near, only the mighty barrows, overgrown with wild thyme and a thousand other flowers, which rise over the graves of the gods. In the tomb of Odin the Government still gives the mead, which was the nectar of Scandinavian heroes, to pilgrim visitors.

Like most of the Swedish towns, Upsala is disappointing, and its mean, ill-paved streets show few signs of antiquity. At the east end of the cathedral is the lofty tomb of Gustavus Wasa, the first Protestant King of Sweden, whose effigy lies between the charming figures of his two pretty little wives. In 1519 he was carried off as a hostage by that Christian, King of Denmark, who forcibly made himself King of Sweden also, and ruled with savage tyranny. Escaping to Lubeck, he headed a revolutionary party against the tyrant, and, after many defeats, succeeded in taking Stockholm, where he was made king in 1523. Soon after, Olaf Petri's translation of the New Testament led to the Reformation in Sweden, where Gustavus Wasa was another Henry VIII., in taking the opportunity of seizing two-thirds of the Church revenues, and depriving all ecclesiastics of their incomes if they refused to embrace Lutheranism. One of his daughters-in-law was the famous Polish princess, Queen Catherine Jagellonica, who tried hard to upset the new religion, and inculcated Catholicism upon her son, King Sigismund, who was deposed, on religious grounds, in favour of his uncle, Charles IX., the father of Gustavus Adolphus. This Queen Catherine Jagel-

Ionica has a fine tomb in a side chapel of Upsala Cathedral.

On a brilliant July morning we embarked at Stockholm in the steamer which runs twice a week down Lake Malar to Gripsholm. Most lovely were the long

GRIPSHOLM.

reaches of still water with their fringe of russet rocks, every crevice tufted with birch and dwarf mountain ash, opening here and there to show some red timber houses or a wooden spire. It was several hours of soft diorama, with the music of the pines, before the great castle of Gripsholm, the Windsor of Sweden, came in sight, with its many red towers and Eastern-looking domes and cupolas. We were landed at the little pier of Mariefred, in itself a lovely scene, with old trees feathering into the water, and a picturesque church rising in a grove of walnuts on a green hill behind. Hard by is a little inn where the whole of the passengers in the steamer dined together, at many little tables, the great staple of food being fresh trout and salmon of the lake, the bilberries and cloudberries of the rocks, and the birch brandy and wild strawberries from the woods. After dinner every one trooped along the meadow paths to the castle, and rambled in friendly companionship over its numerous rooms, full of interest, and with many curious royal portraits and pieces of ancient furniture. There are endless historic recollections connected with Gripsholm, but they centre for the most part around the sons of Gustavus Wasa. Of these, John was immured here by Eric XIV., with his wife Catherine Jagellonica, who, during her imprisonment, gave birth to her son Sigismund (afterwards Sigismund III. of Poland), in a box-bed which still remains. Eric intended to have put his brother to death, but when he entered his cell for the purpose was so overcome by fraternal feeling that he begged his pardon instead. That pardon was not granted, for when John got the upper hand he imprisoned Eric in a small chamber at the top of the castle, where he languished for ten years, during which he wrote a treatise on military art, and translated the history of Johannes Magnus, and where—in the end—he was poisoned.

IN NORWAY

IN NORWAY.

THE weather changed to a cloudless sunshine, which hatched all the mosquitoes, as we entered Norway in the second week in July, and the heat was so intense that, in the long railway journey from Stockholm, we were very thankful for the little tank of iced water with which each railway carriage is provided. We were disappointed in Kristiania, which is a very dull place. The town was built by Christian IV. of Denmark, and has a good central church of his time, but it is utterly unpicturesque. In the picture gallery are several noble works of Tidemann, the special painter of expression and pathos. As a companion for life is the memory of a picture which represents the administration of the last sacrament to an old peasant, whose wife's grief is turned to resignation, which ceases even to have a wish for his retention, as she beholds the heaven-born comfort with which he is looking into an unknown future. Another of the finest works of the artist represents the reception of the sacrament by a convict, young and deeply repentant, before his execution.

There is no striking scenery in the environs of Kristiania, but they are wonderfully pretty. From the avenues upon the ramparts you look down over the broad expanse of the fyord, with low blue mountain distances. Little steamers dart backwards and forwards, and convey visitors in a few minutes across the bay to Oscars Halle, a tower and small country villa of the king on a wooded knoll.

We went by the railway which winds high amongst the hills to Kongsberg, a mining village in a lofty situation. Here, in a garden of white roses, there is a most comfortable small hotel kept by a Dane, which is a capital starting-point for all expeditions in Telemarken. There is a pretty waterfall near the village, and the church should be visited, for the sake of its curious pulpit hour-glass—indeed, four glasses—quarter, half-hour, three-quarters, hour — and the top of a stool let into the wall with an inscription saying that Mr. Jacobus Stuart, King of Scotland (James I. of England), sate upon it, Nov. 25, 1589, to hear a sermon preached by Mr. David Lentz, 'between 11 and 12,' on 'The Lord is my Shepherd.'

We engaged a carriage at Kongsberg for the excursion to Tinoset, whence we arranged to go on to the Ryukan Foss, said to be the highest waterfall in Europe. We do not advise future travellers without unlimited time to follow us in the latter part of the expedition by the lake, but the carriage excursion is quite enchanting. What an exquisite drive it is through the forest—the deep ever-varying woods of noble pines and firs springing from luxuriant thickets of junipers, bilberries, and cranberries! The loveliest mountain flowers grow in these woods—huge larkspurs of rank luxuriant foliage and flowers of faint dead blue; pinks and blue lungworts and orchids; stagmoss wreathing itself round the grey rocks, and delicate, lovely soldanella drooping in the still recesses.

Our midday halt was at Bolkesjö, where the forest opens to green lawns, hill-set, with a charming view down the smooth declivities to a many-bayed lake, with mountain distances. Here, amid a group of old brown farm-buildings covered with rude paintings and sculpture, is a farmhouse, inhabited by the same family through many generations. It is one of the 'stations' where it is part of the duty of the farmer or 'bonder' who is owner of the soil to find horses for the use of travellers. These horses are supplied at a very trifling charge, and are brought back by a boy who sits behind the carriole or carriage upon the portmanteau: but as the horses, when not called for, are turned loose or used by the bonder in his own farm or field work, travellers generally have to wait a long time while they are caught or sent for. They order their horses '*strax*'—directly—one of the first words an Englishman learns to use on entering Norway, yet they scarcely ever appear before half an hour, so that Norwegians repeat with amusement the story of an Englishman who, when he wished to spend an hour at a station, ordered his horses 'after two strax's.' These halts are not always congenial to English impatience, yet they give opportunities of becoming acquainted with Norwegian life and people which can be obtained in no other way, and recollection will oftener go back to the quiet time spent in waiting for horses amid the grey rocks above some foaming streamlet, in the green oases surrounded by forest, or in clean-boarded rooms strewn with fresh fir foliage, than to the more established sights of Norway. Most delicious indeed were the two hours which we passed at Bolkesjö, in the high pastures where the peasants were mowing the tall grass ablaze with flowers, and the mountains were throwing long purple shadows over the forest, and the wind blowing freshly from the gleaming lake—and then, most delicious was the well-earned meal of eggs and bacon, strawberries and cream, and other homely dainties in the farmhouse where the beams and furniture were all painted and carved with mottoes and texts, and the primitive box-beds had crimson satin quilts. Portraits sent by well-pleased royal visitors hung on the walls side by side with common-coloured scripture prints, like those which are found in English cottages. The cellar is under a bed, beneath which it was funny to see the

BOLKESJÖ.

old farmeress disappear as she went down to fetch up for us her home-brewed ale.

With the cordial 'likkelie reise' of our old hostess in our ears, we left Bolkesjö full of pleasant thoughts. But what roads, or rather what want of roads, lead to Tinoset!—there were banks of glassy rock, up which our horses scrambled like cats; there were awful moments when everything seemed to come to an end.

and when they gathered up their legs, and seemed to fling themselves down headlong with the carriage on the top of them, and yet we reached the bottom of the abyss buried in dust, to rise gasping and gulping and wondering we were alive, to begin the same pantomime over again.

Late in the evening, long after the sunlight had faded, and when the forests seemed to have gone to sleep and all sounds were silent, we reached Tinoset. The inn is a wooden châlet on the banks of a lake with a single great pine-tree close to the door. It was terribly crowded, and the little wooden cells were the smallest apology for bedrooms, where all through the night we heard the winds howling among the mountains, and the waves lashing the shore under the windows. In the morning the lake was covered with huge blue waves crested with foam, and we were almost sorry when the steamer came and we felt obliged to embark, because, as it was not the regular day for its passage, we had summoned it at some expense from the other end of the lake. We were thoroughly wet with the spray before we reached the little inn at Strand, with a pier where we disembarked, and occupied the rest of the afternoon in drawing the purple hills, and the road winding towards them through the old birch-trees. An excursion to the

Ryukan Foss occupied the next day; a dull drive through the plain, and then an exciting skirting of horrible precipices, followed by a clamber up a mountain pathlet to a châlet, where we were thankful for our well-earned dinner of trout and ale before proceeding to the Foss, the 560-feet-high fall of a

OLD CHURCH OF HITTERDAL.

mountain torrent into a black rift in the hills—a boiling, roaring abyss of water, with drifts of spray which are visible for miles before it can be seen itself.

In returning from Tinoset, we took the way by Hitterdal, the date-forgotten old wooden church so

I

familiar from picture-books. It had been our principal object in coming to Norway, yet the long drive had made us so ravenous in search of food that we could only endure to stay there half an hour. The church, however, is most intensely picturesque, rising with an infinity of quaintest domes and spires, all built of timber, out of a rude cloister painted red, the whole having the appearance of a very tall Chinese pagoda, yet only measuring altogether 84 feet by 57. The belfry, Norwegian-wise, stands alone on the other side of the churchyard, which is overgrown with pink willow-herb. When we reached the inn, as famished as wolves in winter, we were told by our landlady that she could not give us any dinner. 'Nei, nei,' nothing would induce her—she had too much work on her hands already—perhaps, however, the woman at the house with the flag would give us some. So, hungry and faint, we walked forth again to a house which had a flag flying in front of it, where all was silent and deserted, except for a dog who received us furiously. Having pacified him, and finding the front door locked, we made good our entrance at the back, examined the kitchen, peeped into all the cupboards, lifted up the lids of all the saucepans, and not till we had searched every corner for food ineffectually, were met by the pretty, pleasant-looking young lady of the house, who informed us in excellent English, and with no small surprise at our conduct, that we had been committing a raid upon her private residence. Afterwards we discovered a lonely farmhouse, where there had once been a flag, and where they gave us a very good dinner, ending in a great bowl of cloud-berries—in which we were joined by two pleasant

THRONDTJEM FYORD.

young ladies and their father, an old gentleman smoking an enormous long pipe, who turned out to be the Bishop of Christiansand. The house of the landamann of Hitterdal contains a relic connected with a picturesque story quaintly illustrative of ancient Scandinavian life. It is an axe, with a handle projecting beyond the blade, and curved, so that it can be used as a walking-stick. Formerly it belonged to an ancient descendant of the Kongen, or chieftains of the district, who insisted upon carrying it to church with him in accordance with an old privilege. The priest forbade the bearing of the warlike weapon into church, which so much affected the old man that he died. His son, who thought it necessary to avenge his father's death, went to the priest with the axe in his hands, and demanded the most precious thing he possessed—when the priest brought his Bible and gave it to him, open upon a passage exhorting to forgiveness of injuries.

On July 25 we left Kristiania for Throndtjem—the whole journey of three hundred and sixty miles being very comfortable, and only costing 30 francs. The route has no great beauty, but endless pleasant variety—rail to Eidswold, with bilberries and strawberries in pretty birch-bark baskets for sale at all the railway stations; a vibrating steamer for several hours on the long, dull Miosen lake; railway again, with some of the carriages open at the sides; then an obligatory night at Koppang, a large station, where accommodation is provided for every one, but where, if there are many passengers, several people, strangers to each other, are expected to share the same room. On the second day the scenery improves, the railway sometimes running along and sometimes over the river

Glommen, on a wooden causeway, till the gorge of mountains opens beyond Stören, into a rich country with turfy mounds constantly reminding us of the graves of the hero-gods of Upsala. Towards sunset, beyond the deep cleft in which the river Nid runs between lines of old painted wooden warehouses, rises

THRONDTJEM CATHEDRAL.

the burial-place of S. Olaf, the shrine of Scandinavian Christianity, the stumpy-towered cathedral of Throndtjem. The most northern railway station and the most northern cathedral in Europe!

Surely the cradle of Scandinavian Christianity is one of the most beautiful places in the world! No one had ever told us about it, and we went there only because it is the old Throndtjem of sagas and ballads, and expecting a wonderful and beautiful cathedral. But the whole place is a dream of loveliness, so exquisite in the soft silvery morning light on the fyord and delicate mountain ranges, the rich nearer hills covered with bilberries and breaking into steep cliffs —that one remains in a state of transport, which is at a climax while all is engraven upon an opal sunset sky, when an amethystine glow spreads over the mountains, and when ships and buildings meet their double in the still, transparent water. Each wide street of curious low wooden houses displays a new vista of sea, of rocky promontories, of woods dipping into the water ; and at the end of the principal street is the grey massive cathedral where S. Olaf is buried, and where northern art and poetry have exhausted their loveliest and most pathetic fancies around the grave of the national hero.

The 'Cathedral Garden,' for so the graveyard is called, is most touching. Acres upon acres of graves are all kept—not by officials, but by the families they belong to—like gardens. The tombs are embowered in roses and honeysuckle, and each little green mound has its own vase for cut flowers daily replenished, and a seat for the survivors, which is daily occupied, so that the link between the dead and the living is never broken.

Christianity was first established in Norway at the end of the tenth century by King Olaf Trygveson, son of Trygve and of the lady Astrida, whose romantic adventures, when sold as a slave after her husband's death, are the subject of a thousand stories. When Olaf succeeded to the throne of Norway after the death of Hako, son of Sigurd, in 996, he proclaimed Christianity throughout his dominions, heard matins daily himself, and sent out missionaries through his dominions. But the duty of the so-called missionaries had little to do with teaching, they were only required to baptize. All who refused baptism were tortured and put to death. When, at one time, the estates of the province of Throndtjem tried to force Olaf back to the old religion, he outwardly assented, but made the condition that the offended pagan deities should in that case be appeased by human sacrifice—the sacrifice of the twelve nobles who were most urgent in compelling him; and upon this the ardour of the chieftains for paganism was cooled, and they allowed Olaf unhindered to demolish the great statue of Thor, covered with gold and jewels, in the centre of the province of Throndtjem, where he founded the city then called Nidares, upon the river Nid.

No end of stories are narrated of the cruelties of

Olaf Trygveson. When Egwind, a northern chieftain, refused to abandon his idols, he first attempted to bribe him, but, when gentler means failed, a chafing-dish of hot coals was placed upon his belly till he died. Raude the magician had a more horrible fate: an adder was forced down a horn into his stomach, and left to eat its way out again!

The first Christian king of Norway was an habitual drunkard, and, by twofold adultery, he, the husband of Godruna, married Thyra of Denmark, the wife of Duke Borislaf of Pomerania. This led to a war with Denmark and Sweden, whose united fleets surrounded him near Stralsund. As much mystery enshrouds the story of his death as is connected with that of Arthur, Barbarossa, or Harold: as his royal vessel, the *Long Serpent*, was boarded by the enemy, he plunged into the sea and was no more seen, though some chroniclers say that he swam to the shore in safety and died afterwards at Rome, whither he went on pilgrimage.

Olaf Trygveson had a godson Olaf, son of Harald Grenske and Asta, who had the nominal title of king given to all sea captains of royal descent. From his twelfth year, Olaf Haraldsen was a pirate, and he headed the band of Danes who destroyed Canterbury and murdered S. Elphege—a strange feature in the life of one who has been himself regarded as a saint since his death. By one of the strange freaks of fortune common in those times, this Olaf Haraldsen gained a great victory over the chieftain Sweyn, who then ruled at Nidaros, and, chiefly through the influence of Sigurd Syr, a great northern landowner who had become the second husband of his mother, he became seated in 1016 upon the throne of Norway. His first care was for the restoration of Christianity, which had fallen into decadence in the sixteen years which had elapsed since the defeat of Olaf Trygveson. The second Olaf imitated the violence and cruelty of his predecessor. Whenever the new religion was rejected, he beheaded or hung the delinquents. In his most merciful moments he mutilated and blinded them: 'he did not spare one who refused to serve God.' After fourteen years of unparalleled cruelties in the name of religion, he fell in battle with Canute the Great at Sticklestadt. He had abducted and married Astrida, daughter of the King of Sweden, but by her he had no children. By his concubine Alfhilda he left an only son, who lived to become Magnus the Good, King of Norway. There is a very fine story of the way in which Magnus obtained his name. Olaf had said, 'I very seldom sleep, and if I ever do it will be the worse for any one who awakens me.' Whilst he was asleep Alfhilda's child was born. Then the King's scald or poet and Siegfried the mass priest debated together as to whether they should awaken him. At first they thought they would; then the poet said, 'No; I know him better than that: he must not be awakened.' 'That is all very well,' said the priest, 'but the child must be baptised at once. What shall we call him?' 'Oh,' said the scald, 'I know that the King said that the child should be named after the greatest monarch that ever lived, and his name was Magnus,' for he only remembered one part of the name. So they called him Magnus.

When the King woke up he was furious. 'Who can have dared to do this thing—to christen the child without consulting me, and to give him this outlandish name, which is no name at all—who can have dared to do it?'

Then the mass priest was terrified and shrank into his shoes, but the scald answered boldly, 'I did it, and I did it because it was better to send two souls to God than one soul to the devil; for if the child had died unbaptised it would have been lost, but if you kill Siegfried and me we shall go straight to heaven.'

And then King Olaf thought he would say no more about it.

However terrible the cruelties of Olaf Haraldsen were in his lifetime, they were soon dazzled out of sight amid the halo of miracles with which his memory was encircled by the Roman Catholic Church. It was only recollected that when, according to the legend, he raced for the kingdom with his half-brother Harald, in his good ship the *Ox*,

> Saint Olaf, who on God relied,
> Three days the first his house descried ;

after which

> Harald so fierce with anger burned
> He to a lothely dragon turned ;

but because

> A pious zeal Saint Olaf bore,
> He long the crown of Norway wore.

His admirers narrated that when he was absently cutting chips from a stick with his knife on a Sunday, a servant passed him with the reproof, 'Sir, it is Monday to-morrow,' when he placed the sinful chips in his hand, and, setting them on fire, bore the pain till they were all consumed. It was remembered that as he walked to the church which Olaf Trygveson had founded at Nidaros, he 'wore a glory in h's yellow hair.' And gradually he became the most popular saint of Scandinavia. His shirt was an object of pilgrimage in the Church of S. Victor at Paris, and many churches were dedicated to him in England, and especially in London, where Tooley Street still records his familiar appellation of S. Tooley.

It was when the devotion to S. Olaf was just beginning that Earl Godwin and his sons were banished from England for a time. Two of these, Harold and Tosti, became vikings, and, in a great battle, they vowed that, if they were victorious, they would give half the spoil to the shrine of S. Olaf; and a huge silver statue, which they actually gave, existed at Throndtjem till 1500, and if it existed still would be one of the most important relics in archæology. The old Kings of Norway used to dig up the saint from time to time and cut his nails. When Harold Hardrada was going to England, he declared that he must see S. Olaf once again. 'I must see my brother once more,' he said, and he also cut the saint's nails. But he also thought that from that time it would be better that no one should see his brother any more—it would not be for the good of the Church—so he took the keys of the shrine and threw them into the fyord; at the same time however, he said it would be good for men in after-ages to know what a great king was like, so he caused S. Olaf's measure to be engraved upon the wall in the church at Throndtjem—his measure of seven feet—and there it is still.

Around the shrine of Olaf in Throndtjem, in which, in spite of Harold Hardrada, his 'incorrupt

S. OLAF'S WELL.

body' was seen more than five hundred years after his death, has arisen the most beautiful of northern cathedrals, originating in a small chapel built over his grave within ten years after his death. The exquisite colour of its green-grey stone adds greatly to the general effect of the interior, and to the delicate sculpture of its interlacing arches. From the ambulatory behind the choir opens a tiny chamber containing the Well of S. Olaf, of rugged yellow stone, with the holes remaining in the pavement through which the dripping water ran away when the buckets were set down. Amongst the many famous Bishops of Throndtjem, perhaps the most celebrated has been Anders Arrebo, 'the father of Danish poetry' (1587–1637), who wrote the 'Hexameron,' an extraordinarily long poem on the Creation, which nobody reads now. The cathedral is given up to Lutheran worship, but its ancient relics are kindly tended and cared for, and the building is being beautifully restored. Its beautiful Chapter House is lent for English service on Sundays.

In the wide street which leads from the sea to the cathedral is the 'Coronation House,' the wooden palace in which the Kings and Queens of Sweden and Norway stay when they come hither to be crowned. Hither the present beloved Queen, Sophie of Nassau, came in 1873, driving herself in her own carriole from the Romsdal, in graceful compliance with the popular mode of Norwegian travel. It is because even the finest buildings in Norway are generally built of wood that there are so few of any real antiquity. Near the shore of the fyord, the custom-house occupies the site of the Orething, where the elections of twenty kings have taken place. It is sacred ground to a King of Norway, who passes it bareheaded. The familiar affection with which the Norwegians regard their sovereigns can scarcely be comprehended in any other country. To their people they are 'the father and mother of the land.' The broken Norse is remembered at Throndtjem in which King Carl Johann begged people 'to make room for their old father' when they pressed too closely upon him. When the present so beloved Queen drove herself to her coronation, the people met her with flowers at all the 'stations' where the horses were changed. 'Are you the mother of the land?' they said. 'You look nice, but you must do more than look nice; that is not the essential.' One old woman begged the lady in waiting to beg her majesty to get upon the roof of the house. 'Then we should all see her.' At Throndtjem the peasants touchingly and affectionately always addressed her as 'Du.'

In returning from Throndtjem we left the railway at Stören, where we engaged a double carriole, and a carriage for four with a pleasant boy called Johann as its driver, for the return journey. It was difficult to obtain definite information about anything, English books being almost useless from their incorrectness, and we set off with a sort of sense of exploring an unknown country. At every 'station' we changed horses, which were sent back by the boy, who perched upon the luggage behind, and we marked our distances by calling our horses after the Kings of England. Thus, setting off from Stören with William the Conqueror, we drove into the Romsdal with Edward VI. After a drive with Lady Jane Grey, we set off again with Mary. But the Kings of England failed us long before our driving days were over, and we used up all the Kings of Rome also. As we were coming down a steep hill into Lillehammer with Tarquinius Superbus, something gave way and he quietly walked out of the harness, leaving us to run briskly down-hill and subside into the hedge. We captured Tarquinius, but how to put him in again was a mystery, as we had never harnessed a horse before. However, by trying every strap in turn we got him in somehow, and escaped the fate of Red Riding Hood amid the lonely hills.

For a great distance after leaving Stören there is little especially striking in the scenery, except one gorge of old weird pine-trees in a rift of purple mountains. After you emerge upon the high Dovre-Fyeld, the huge ranges of Snechatten rise snowy, gleaming, and glorious, above the wide yellow-grey expanse, hoary with reindeer moss, though, as the Dovre-Fyeld is itself three thousand feet high, and Snechatten only seven thousand three hundred, it does not look so high as it really is. Next to Throndtjem itself, the old ballads and songs of Norway gather most thickly around the Dovre-Fyeld. It is here that the witches are supposed to hold their secret meetings at their Blokulla, or black hill. Across these yellow hills of the Jerkin-Fyeld the prose Edda describes Thor striding to his conflict with the dragon Jormangandur 'by Snechatten's peak of snow,' where 'the tall pines cracked like a field of stubble under his feet;' and here, according to the ancient fragment called the ballad of 'The Twelve Wizards,' as given in Prior's 'Ancient Danish Ballads'—

> At Dovrefeld, over on Norway's reef,
> Were heroes who never knew pain or grief.
>
> There dwelt there many a warrior keen,
> The twelve bold brothers of Ingeborg queen.
>
> The first with his hand the storm could hush
> The second could stop the torrent's rush.

The third could dive in the sea as a fish;
The fourth never wanted meat on dish.

The fifth he would strike the golden lyre,
And young and old to the dancing fire.

The sixth on the horn would blow a blast,
Who heard it would shudder and stand aghast.

The seventh go under the earth could he;
The eighth he could dance on the rolling sea.

The ninth tamed all that in greenwood crept;
The tenth not a nap had ever slept.

The eleventh the grisly lindworm bound,
And will what he would, the means he found.

The twelfth he could all things understand,
Though done in a nook of the farthest land.

Their equals were never seen there in the North,
Nor anywhere else on the face of the earth.

In spite of great fatigue from the distances to be accomplished, each day's journey in carriage or carriole has its peculiar charms, the going on and on into an unknown land, meeting no one, sleeping in odd, primitive, but always clean rooms, setting off again at half-past five or six, and halting at comfortable stations, with their ever-moderate prices and their cheery farm-servants, who kissed our hands all round on receiving the very smallest gratuity—a coin meaning twopence-halfpenny being a source of ecstatic bliss.

The 'bonders,' who keep the stations, generally themselves represent the gentry of the country, the real gentry filling the position of the English aristocracy. The bonders are generally very well off, having small tithes, good houses, boundless fuel, a great variety of food, and continual change of labour on their own small properties. Their wives, who never walk, have a sledge for winter, and a carriole and horse to take them to church in summer. In the many months of snow, when the cows and horses are all stabled in the 'laave,' and when out-of-door occupations fail, they occupy the time with household pursuits—carpentering, tailoring, or brewing. When a bonder dies, his wife succeeds to his property until her second marriage; then it is divided amongst his children.

The 'stations' or farmhouses are almost entirely built of wood, but those of a superior class have a single room of stone, used only in bridals or births, a custom handed down from old times when a place of special safety was required at those seasons.

Nine-tenths of the country are covered with pine-forests, but the trees are always cut down before they grow old. We did not see a single old tree in Norway. The pines are of two kinds only—the *Furu*, our pine, *Pinus silvestris*; and the *Gran*, our fir, *Pinus abies*.

Wolves seldom appear except in winter, when those who travel in sledges are often pursued by them. Then hunger makes them so bold that they will often snatch a dog from between the knees of a driver.

From the station of Dombaas (where there is a telegraph station and a shop of old silver) we turned aside down the Romsdal, which soon became beautiful, as the road wound above the chrysoprase river Rauma, broken by many rocky islets and swirling into many waterfalls, but always equally radiant, equally transparent, till its colour is washed out by the melting snow in a ghastly narrow valley, which we called the Valley of Death.

The little inn at Aak, in Romsdal, with a large garden stretching along the hillside, disappointed us at first, as the clouds hid the mountain-tops, but morning revealed how glorious they are—purple pinnacles of rock or pathless fields of snow embossed upon a sky which is delicately blue above but melts into the clearest opal. Grander, we thought, than any single peak in Switzerland is the tremendous peak of the Romsdalhorn, and the walks in all directions are most exquisite—into deep glades filled with columbines and the giant larkspurs, which are such a feature of Norway : into tremendous mountain gorges : or to Waeblungsnaes, along the banks of the lovely fyord, with its marvellously quaint forms of mountain distance. Aak is a place where a month

IN THE ROMSDAL, NORWAY.

may be spent most delightfully, as well as most comfortably and economically.

We had heard a great deal before we went to Norway about the difficulty of getting proper food, but our own experience is that we were never fed more luxuriously. Perhaps very late in the season the provisions at the country 'stations' may be somewhat used up, but when we were there in July only those who could not live without a great deal of meat could have any cause for complaint, and once a week we generally had reindeer for a treat. When we arrived in the evenings, we always found an excellent meal prepared—the most delicious coffee, tea, and cream; baskets of bread, rusks, cakes and biscuits of various descriptions; fresh salmon and trout; cloudberries, bilberries, raspberries, mountain strawberries and cream; and for all this about a franc and a half is the payment required.

My companions lingered at Kristiania whilst I paid a visit, which is one of the most delightful recollections of my tour, to a native family near Moss, at the mouth of the fyord; then we came back to Denmark, travelling in the same train with the beloved Prince Imperial, who was then in the height of health and happiness, and received at every station with the enthusiastic 'Hochs!' which in Scandinavia supply the place of the English hurrah.

WORKS BY AUGUSTUS J. C. HARE.

CITIES OF SOUTHERN ITALY AND SICILY.
With Illustrations. Crown 8vo. 10s. 6d.

'Mr. Hare's name will be a sufficient passport for the popularity of his new work. His books on the Cities of Italy are fast becoming as indispensable to the traveller in that part of the country as the guide-books of Murray or of Baedeker......His book is one which I should advise all future travellers in Southern Italy and Sicily to find room for in their portmanteaus.'—ACADEMY.

'We regard the volume as a necessary part of the equipment of a traveller in Southern Italy; if he goes without it he will miss the most thorough and most helpful book that has treated it. The part devoted to Sicily is especially full of interest; and we should not omit to make mention of the exquisite little woodcuts done from Mr. Hare's water-colours executed on the spot.'—BRITISH QUARTERLY REVIEW.

CITIES OF CENTRAL ITALY. With Illustrations.
2 vols. crown 8vo. 21s.

CITIES OF NORTHERN ITALY. With Illustrations.
2 vols. crown 8vo. 21s.

'We can imagine no better way of spending a wet day in Florence or Venice than in reading all that Mr. Hare has to say and quote about the history, arts, and famous people of those cities. These volumes come under the class of volumes not to borrow, but to buy.'—MORNING POST.

WALKS IN ROME. Eleventh Edition. With Map.
2 vols. crown 8vo. 18s.

'The best handbook of the city and environs of Rome ever published...... Cannot be too much commended.'—PALL MALL GAZETTE.

'This book is sure to be very useful. It is thoroughly practical, and is the best guide that yet has been offered.'—DAILY NEWS.

'Mr. Hare's book fills a real void, and gives to the tourist all the latest discoveries and the fullest information bearing on that most inexhaustible of subjects, the city of Rome...... It is much fuller than "Murray," and anyone who chooses may now know how Rome really looks in sun or shade.'—SPECTATOR.

WALKS IN LONDON. Fifth Edition. With numerous Illustrations.
2 vols. crown 8vo. 21s.

'One of the really valuable as well as pleasant companions to the peripatetic philosopher's rambling studies of the town.'—DAILY TELEGRAPH.

DAYS NEAR ROME. With more than 100 Illustrations
by the Author. Third Edition. 2 vols. crown 8vo. 24s.

London: SMITH, ELDER, & CO., 15 Waterloo Place.

Works by Augustus J. C. Hare.

WANDERINGS IN SPAIN. With Illustrations. Fourth Edition. Crown 8vo. 7s. 6d.

'Mr. Hare's book is admirable. We are sure no one will regret making it the companion of a Spanish journey. It will bear reading repeatedly when one is moving among the scenes it describes—no small advantage when the travelling library is scanty.'—SATURDAY REVIEW.

'Here is the ideal book of travel in Spain: the book which exactly anticipates the requirements of everybody who is fortunate enough to be going to that enchanted land; the book which ably consoles those who are not so happy by supplying the imagination from the daintiest and most delicious of its stories.'
SPECTATOR.

'Since the publication of "Castilian Days," by the American diplomat, Mr. John Hay, no pleasanter or more readable sketches have fallen under our notice.'
ATHENÆUM.

THE LIFE AND LETTERS OF FRANCES BARONESS BUNSEN. With Portraits. 2 vols. crown 8vo. 24s.

MEMORIALS OF A QUIET LIFE. 3 vols. crown 8vo. Vols. I. and II. 21s.; Vol. III., with numerous Photographs, 10s. 6d.

'The name of Hare is one deservedly to be honoured; and in these "Memorials," which are as true and satisfactory a biography as it is possible to write, the author places his readers in the heart of the family, and allows them to see the hidden sources of life and love by which it is nourished and sustained.'—ATHENÆUM.

'One of those books which it is impossible to read without pleasure. It conveys a sense of repose not unlike that which everybody must have felt out of service time in quiet little village churches. Its editor will receive the hearty thanks of every cultivated reader for these profoundly interesting "Memorials" of two brothers, whose names and labours their universities and church have alike reason to cherish with affection and remember with pride, who have smoothed the path of faith to so many troubled wayfarers, strengthening the weary and confirming the weak.'
STANDARD.

'The book is rich in insight and in contrast of character. It is varied and full of episodes, which few can fail to read with interest; and as exhibiting the sentiments and thoughts of a very influential circle of minds during a quarter of a century, it may be said to have a distinct historical value.'—NONCONFORMIST.

'A charming book, simply and gracefully recording the events of simple and gracious life. Its connection with the beginning of a great movement in the English Church will make it to the thoughtful reader more profoundly suggestive than many biographies crowded and bustling with incident. It is almost the first of a class of books the Christian world just now greatly needs, as showing how the spiritual life was maintained amid the shaking of religious "opinions"; how the life of the soul deepened as the thoughts of the mind broadened; and how, in their union, the two formed a volume of larger and more thoroughly vitalised Christian idea than the English people had witnessed for many days.'—GLASGOW HERALD.

FLORENCE. Fcp. 8vo. cloth limp, 2s. 6d.

VENICE. Fcp. 8vo. cloth limp, 2s. 6d.

London: SMITH, ELDER, & CO., 15 Waterloo Place.

WORKS BY AUGUSTUS J. C. HARE

LIFE AND LETTERS OF FRANCES, BARONESS BUNSEN. *Fourth Edition.* With Portraits. 2 vols., crown 8vo, Cloth, 21s.

MEMORIALS OF A QUIET LIFE. 3 vols., crown 8vo. Vols. I. and II., Cloth, 21s. (*Nineteenth Edition*); Vol. III., with numerous Photographs, Cloth, 10s. 6d.

"One of those books which it is impossible to read without pleasure. It conveys a sense of repose not unlike that which everybody must have felt out of service time in quiet little village churches. Its editor will receive the hearty thanks of every cultivated reader for these profoundly interesting 'Memorials' of two brothers, whose names and labours their universities and Church have alike reason to cherish with affection and remember with pride, who have smoothed the path of faith to so many troubled wayfarers, strengthening the weary and confirming the weak."—*Standard.*

DAYS NEAR ROME. With more than 100 Illustrations by the Author. *Third Edition.* 2 vols., crown 8vo, Cloth, 7s. 6d.

WALKS IN ROME. *Sixteenth Edition.* Revised by the AUTHOR and ST. CLAIR BADDELEY. With 3 Plans and Illustrations showing recent discoveries. 2 vols., fcap. 8vo, Cloth limp, 10s. 6d.

"The best handbook of the city and environs of Rome ever published. . . . Cannot be too much commended."—*Pall Mall Gazette.*

"This book is sure to be very useful. It is thoroughly practical, and is the best guide that has yet been offered."—*Daily News.*

"Mr. Hare's book fills a real void, and gives to the tourist all the latest discoveries and the fullest information bearing on that most inexhaustible of subjects, the city of Rome. . . . It is much fuller than 'Murray,' and any one who chooses may know how Rome really looks in sun or shade."—*Spectator.*

WALKS IN LONDON. *Seventh Edition, revised.* With additional Illustrations. 2 vols., fcap. 8vo, Cloth limp, 12s.

"One of the really valuable as well as pleasant companions to the peripatetic philosopher's rambling studies of the town."—*Daily Telegraph.*

WESTMINSTER. Reprinted from "Walks in London," as a Handy Guide. *Third Edition.* 120 pages. Paper Covers, 6d. net; Cloth, 1s.

WANDERINGS IN SPAIN. With 17 Full-page Illustrations. *Eighth Edition.* Fcap. 8vo, Cloth limp, 3s.

"Here is the ideal book of travel in Spain; the book which exactly anticipates the requirements of everybody who is fortunate enough to be going to that enchanted land; the book which ably consoles those who are not so happy by supplying the imagination from the daintiest and most delicious of its stories."—*Spectator.*

GEORGE ALLEN, 156, CHARING CROSS ROAD, LONDON

CITIES OF SOUTHERN ITALY AND SICILY.
With Illustrations. Crown 8vo, Cloth, 10s. 6d.

"Mr. Hare's name will be a sufficient passport for the popularity of his work. His books on the Cities of Italy are fast becoming as indispensable to the traveller in that part of the country as the guide-books of Murray or of Baedeker. . . . His book is one which I should advise all future travellers in Southern Italy and Sicily to find room for in their portmanteaus."—*Academy.*

CITIES OF NORTHERN ITALY. *Second Edition.*
With Illustrations. 2 vols., crown 8vo, Cloth, 7s. 6d.

"We can imagine no better way of spending a wet day in Florence or Venice than in reading all that Mr. Hare has to say and quote about the history, arts, and famous people of those cities. These volumes come under the class of volumes not to borrow, but to buy."—*Morning Post.*

CITIES OF CENTRAL ITALY. *Second Edition.* With Illustrations. 2 vols., crown 8vo, Cloth, 7s. 6d.

SKETCHES IN HOLLAND AND SCANDINAVIA.
Crown 8vo, with Illustrations, Cloth, 3s.

"This little work is the best companion a visitor to these countries can have, while those who stay at home can also read it with pleasure and profit."—*Glasgow Herald.*

STUDIES IN RUSSIA. Crown 8vo, with numerous Illustrations, Cloth, 6s.

"Mr. Hare's book may be recommended as at once entertaining and instructive."—*Athenaeum.*

"A delightful and instructive guide to the places visited. It is, in fact, a sort of glorified guide-book, with all the charm of a pleasant and cultivated literary companion."—*Scotsman.*

FLORENCE. *Sixth Edition.* Revised by the AUTHOR and W. ST. CLAIR BADDELEY. Fcap. 8vo, Cloth limp. 3s. With 2 Plans and 30 Illustrations.

VENICE. *Sixth Edition.* Revised by the AUTHOR and W. ST. CLAIR BADDELEY. Fcap. 8vo, Cloth limp, 3s. With 2 Plans and 17 Illustrations.

"The plan of these little volumes is excellent. . . . Anything more perfectly fulfilling the idea of a guide-book we have never seen."—*Scottish Review.*

THE RIVIERAS. Fcap. 8vo, Cloth limp, 3s. With 67 Illustrations.

PARIS. *New Edition, revised.* With 50 Illustrations. Fcap. 8vo, Cloth limp, 6s. 2 vols., sold separately.

GEORGE ALLEN, 156, CHARING CROSS ROAD, LONDON

WORKS BY AUGUSTUS J. C. HARE

DAYS NEAR PARIS. With Illustrations. Crown 8vo, Cloth, 6s.; or in 2 vols., Cloth limp, 6s. 6d.

NORTH-EASTERN FRANCE. Crown 8vo, Cloth, 6s. With Map and 86 Woodcuts.

Picardy—Abbeville and Amiens—Paris and its Environs—Arras and the Manufacturing Towns of the North—Champagne—Nancy and the Vosges, &c.

SOUTH-EASTERN FRANCE. Crown 8vo, Cloth, 6s. With Map and 176 Woodcuts.

The different lines to the South—Burgundy—Auvergne—The Cantal—Provence—The Alpes Dauphinaises and Alpes Maritimes, &c.

SOUTH-WESTERN FRANCE. Crown 8vo, Cloth, 6s. With Map and 232 Woodcuts.

The Loire—The Gironde and Landes—Creuse—Corrèze—The Limousin—Gascony and Languedoc—The Cevennes and the Pyrenees, &c.

NORTH-WESTERN FRANCE. Crown 8vo, Cloth, 6s. With Map and 73 Woodcuts.

Normandy and Brittany—Rouen—Dieppe—Cherbourg—Bayeux—Caen—Coutances—Chartres—Mont S. Michel—Dinan—Brest—Alençon, &c.

"Mr. Hare's volumes, with their charming illustrations, are a reminder of how much we miss by neglecting provincial France."—*Times.*

"The appreciative traveller in France will find no more pleasant, inexhaustible, and discriminating guide than Mr. Hare. . . . All the volumes are most liberally supplied with drawings, all of them beautifully executed, and some of them genuine masterpieces."—*Echo.*

"Every one who has used one of Mr. Hare's books will welcome the appearance of his new work upon France. . . . The books are the most satisfactory guide-books for a traveller of culture who wishes improvement as well as entertainment from a tour. . . . It is not necessary to go to the places described before the volumes become useful. While part of the work describes the district round Paris, the rest practically opens up a new country for English visitors to provincial France."—*Scotsman.*

SUSSEX. *Second Edition.* With Map and 45 Woodcuts. Crown 8vo, Cloth, 6s.

SHROPSHIRE. With Map and 48 Woodcuts. Cloth, 6s.

LONDON: GEORGE ALLEN, 156, CHARING CROSS ROAD

WORKS BY AUGUSTUS J. C. HARE

THE STORY OF TWO NOBLE LIVES. CHARLOTTE, COUNTESS CANNING, AND LOUISA, MARCHIONESS OF WATERFORD. In 3 vols. Crown 8vo, Cloth, £1, 11s. 6d. Illustrated with 11 engraved Portraits and 21 Plates in Photogravure from Lady Waterford's Drawings, 8 full-page and 24 smaller Woodcuts from Sketches by the Author.

Also a Special Large Paper Edition, with India Proofs of the Plates. Crown 4to, £3, 3s. *net*.

THE GURNEYS OF EARLHAM: Memoirs and Letters of the Eleven Children of JOHN and CATHERINE GURNEY of Earlham, 1775-1875, and the Story of their Religious Life under many Different Forms. Illustrated with 33 Photogravure Plates and 19 Woodcuts. In 2 vols., crown 8vo, Cloth, 25s.

[*Second Edition.*]

BIOGRAPHICAL SKETCHES: Memorial Sketches of ARTHUR PENRHYN STANLEY, Dean of Westminster; HENRY ALFORD, Dean of Canterbury; Mrs. DUNCAN STEWART; and PARAY LE MONIAL. Illustrated with 7 Portraits and 17 Woodcuts. Crown 8vo, Cloth, 6s.

THE STORY OF MY LIFE: 1834 TO 1870. Vols. I. to III. Recollections of Places, People, and Conversations, from Letters and Journals. Illustrated with 18 Photogravure Portraits and 144 Woodcuts from Drawings by the Author. Crown 8vo, Cloth, £1, 11s. 6d.

THE STORY OF MY LIFE: 1870 TO 1900. Vols. IV. to VI. With 12 Photogravure Plates and 247 Woodcuts. Crown 8vo, Cloth, £1, 11s. 6d.

BY THE LATE AUGUSTUS WILLIAM HARE
RECTOR OF ALTON BARNES

THE ALTON SERMONS. *Fifth Edition.* Crown 8vo, 6s.

SERMONS ON THE LORD'S PRAYER. Crown 8vo, 1s. 6d.

GEORGE ALLEN, 156, CHARING CROSS ROAD, LONDON

THE STORY OF MY LIFE

By AUGUSTUS J. C. HARE

Vols. I. to III.   Crown 8vo, £1, 11s. 6d.
Vols. IV. to VI.   Crown 8vo, £1, 11s. 6d.

PRESS NOTICES

"The story is full of varied interest. . . . Readers who know how to pick and choose will find plenty to entertain them, and not a little which is well worth reading."—*The Times.*

"Mr. Hare gives an idyllic picture of the simple, refined, dignified life at Lime. . . . The volumes are an inexhaustible storehouse of anecdote."—*Daily News.*

"The reader rarely comes across a passage which does not afford amusement or pleasant entertainment."—*The Scotsman.*

"One may safely predict that this will be the most popular book of the season. . . . We have not space to point out a twentieth part of the passages that might be described as having a special interest. Moreover, though the book is, among other things, a repertory of curious occurrences and amusing anecdotes, it is much more remarkable as a book of sentiment and character, and a story of real life told with remarkable fulness."—*The Guardian.*

"A book which will greatly amuse the reader."—*The Spectator.*

"Much of what the author has to tell is worthy the telling, and is told with considerable ease and grace, and with a power to interest out of the common. He introduces us to the best of good company, and tells many excellently witty stories. . . .

GEORGE ALLEN, 156, CHARING CROSS ROAD, LONDON

Whenever he is describing foreign life he is at his best: and nothing can exceed the beautiful pathos of the episodes in which his mother appears. Indeed, he has the gift of tenderness for all good women and brave men."—*Daily Telegraph*.

"This autobiography could not fail to be exceptionally interesting. There may be readers who will protest that the more minute details of daily life might have been abridged with advantage, but the aim of the book makes this elaborate treatment of the subject indispensable. The conscientious record of a mental development amid curious surroundings, would make these volumes valuable if not a single name of note were mentioned. . . . Even more interesting than the stories of people and things that are still remembered are the glimpses of a past which is quickly fading out of recollection."—*The Standard*.

"The book is unexceptionable on the score of taste. . . . It is an agreeable miscellany into which one may dip at random with the certainty of landing something entertaining, rather than an autobiography of the ordinary kind. The concluding chapter is full of a deep and tender pathos."—*The Manchester Guardian*.

"Mr. Hare's style is graceful and felicitous, and his life-history was well worth writing. The volumes simply teem with good things, and in a single article we can but skim the surface of the riches they contain. A word must also be said of the beauty and delicacy of the illustrations. Few living men dare brave criticism by giving us the story of their lives and promising more. But Mr. Hare is quite justified. He has produced a fascinating work, in some parts strange as any romance, and his reminiscences of great men are agreeable and interesting."—*Birmingham Gazette*.

GEORGE ALLEN, 156, *CHARING CROSS ROAD, LONDON*

"An inexhaustible storehouse of anecdote."—*South-Western News.*

"These volumes possess an almost unique interest because of the striking series of portraits we get in them, not so much of celebrities, of whom we often hear enough, but of 'originals' in private life. . . . They give us a truly remarkable picture of certain sections of European society, and, above all, introduce us to some singularly quaint types of human character."—*Glasgow Herald.*

"Brimful of anecdotes, this autobiography will yield plenty of entertainment. We should like to quote many a characteristic little tale, but must content ourselves by heartily recommending all who care for the pleasantest of pleasant gossip concerning famous people and places to procure these three volumes."—*Publisher's Circular.*

"Mr. Hare has an easy, agreeable style, and tells a story with humour and skill."—*The Saturday Review.*

"It would be well for all who think the children of to-day are over-pampered and too much considered, to read Mr. Hare's life."—*Lady's Pictorial.*

"Very delicate, idyllic, and fascinating are the pictures the author has drawn of daily life in old rectories and country houses."—*The World.*

"Mr. Hare has the gift, the rare gift, of writing about himself truthfully. Nor can a quick eye for shades of character be denied to Mr. Hare, who does not seem ready to take people at their own estimate or even at what may be called their market price. But we do not detect a touch of malice, but only that knack of telling the truth which is so hateful to the ordinary biographer, and so distasteful to that sentimental public which is never so happy as when devouring sugared falsehoods."—*The Speaker.*

GEORGE ALLEN, 156, *CHARING CROSS ROAD, LONDON*

"The book has throughout a strong human interest. It contains a great many anecdotes, and in our opinion, at all events, deserves to take rank among notable biographical works."—*Westminster Gazette.*

"A deeply interesting book. It is the story of a man who has seen much and suffered much, and who out of the fulness of his experience can bring forth much to interest and entertain. . . . The book has a wealth of apt quotations and graceful reference, and though written in a scholarly and cultured way, it is always simple and interesting. . . . Nothing in the work has been set down in malice; there are excuses for everybody. . . . Of course it is hardly necessary to say that the book teems with entertainment from beginning to end."—*St. James's Budget.*

"There is much besides human character and incident in these well-packed and well-illustrated volumes. . . . No one will close the work without a feeling not only of gratitude for a long gallery of interesting and brilliantly-speaking portraits, but of sympathy with the biographer."—*The Athenæum.*

"It is doubtful whether any Englishman living has had a wider acquaintance among people worth knowing in England and on the Continent, than the author of these memoirs. It is also doubtful whether any man, with equal opportunities, could have turned them to so good an account. . . . We have here an incomparable storehouse of anecdotes concerning conspicuous persons of the first half of this Victorian age."—*New York Sun.*

"This is assuredly a book to read."—*Freeman.*

"Singularly interesting is this autobiography. . . . Altogether it is a notable book, and may well be recommended to those who are interested in the intellectual life of our time."—*New York Herald.*

GEORGE ALLEN, 156, CHARING CROSS ROAD, LONDON

"Mr. Hare's excellence, apart from felicity of style and directness of method, has ever been conspicuous by the excellence that comes of wide knowledge of his subject, and a keenly sympathetic nature. Alive as he has ever been to responsive emotion, he possesses also a bright humour that seizes upon the discrepancies, the nuances and quaintnesses of whatever comes within the range of his eye and pen. These qualities have made for Mr. Hare a circle of admirers who, while they have sought in his pages no very thrilling passages, have felt steadily the growth of a liking given to an old friend who is always kindly and oftentimes amusing. . . . Mr. Hare dwells with a rare and touching love upon his mother, and these passages are amongst the most appealing in the book."—*Philadelphia Courier.*

"Mr. Hare has given us a picture of English social life that for vividness, picturesqueness, and completeness, is not excelled in literature. There is a charming lack of attempt to be literary in the telling of the story—a refreshing frankness and quaintness of expression. He takes his readers with him so that they may breathe the same social atmosphere in which he has spent his life. With their own eyes they see the things he saw, and best of all they have freedom to judge them, for Mr. Hare does not force himself or his opinions upon them."—*New York Press.*

"Mr. Hare's memoirs are their own excuse for being, and are a distinct addition to the wide and delightful realm of biographical literature."—*Chicago Journal.*

"It is rarely that an autobiography is planned on so ample a scale, and yet, to tell the truth, there are singularly few of these pages which one really cares to skip."—*Good Words.*

"A sad history of Mr. Hare's childhood and boyhood this is for the most part, but there were bursts of sunshine in Augustus Hare's life—sunshine shed around him by the kindly, noble-

...minded lady who is called mother all through these volumes, and for whom his reverence and gratitude deepened with years."—*Clifton Society.*

"The 'Story of My Life' is no commonplace autobiography, and plunge in where you may, there is something to interest and attract."—*The Sketch.*

"No one can read these very fascinating pages without feeling that what their author has written is absolutely that which no other would have ventured to say of him, and what not one in a million would have told concerning himself. There is a wonderful charm of sincerity in what he discloses as to his own feelings, his likes and dislikes, his actions and trials. He lays open, with photographic fidelity, the story of his life."—*New York Churchman.*

"These fair volumes might be labelled the Literature of Peace. They offer an outlook on life observant, and yet detached, from the turmoil of disillusion."—*New York Times.*

"Mr. Hare has written an autobiography that will not soon be forgotten."—*Chicago Tribune.*

"The story of Mr. Hare's literary life is most entertaining, and the charm of the work lies pre-eminently in the pictures of the many interesting and often famous men and women whom he has known."—*Boston Congregationalist.*

"Mr. Hare's story is an intensely interesting one, and his style, which at first appears to be diffuse, is soon seen to be perfectly well adapted to the writer's purpose. . . . These volumes are full of the most valuable and attractive material for the student of human nature."—*The Book Buyer.*

"Mr. Hare's story contains no touches of egotism, but is always plain, honest, and straightforward. It is distinctly worth reading."—*London Literary World.*

GEORGE ALLEN, 156, CHARING CROSS ROAD, LONDON

www.ingramcontent.com/pod-product-compliance
Lightning Source LLC
Chambersburg PA
CBHW030342170426
43202CB00010B/1206